100 Ideas for Primary Teachers:

Questioning

Peter Worley

BLOOMSBURY EDUCATION

LONDON   OXFORD   NEW YORK   NEW DELHI   SYDNEY

BLOOMSBURY EDUCATION
Bloomsbury Publishing Plc
50 Bedford Square, London, WC1B 3DP, UK

BLOOMSBURY, BLOOMSBURY EDUCATION and
the Diana logo are trademarks of Bloomsbury Publishing Plc

First published in Great Britain, 2019

A catalogue record for this book is available from the British Library

ISBN: PB: 978-1-4729-5741-2; ePDF: 978-1-4729-5742-9;
ePub: 978-1-4729-5743-6

2 4 6 8 10 9 7 5 3

Typeset by Newgen KnowledgeWorks Pvt. Ltd., Chennai, India
Printed and bound in Great Britain by CPI Group (UK) Ltd, Croydon CR0 4YY

To find out more about our authors and books visit
www.bloomsbury.com and sign up for our newsletters

Contents

Acknowledgements

I would like to thank Hannah Marston at Bloomsbury for a great editing job and the rest of the Bloomsbury team. As always, I owe a debt to The Philosophy Foundation team for their ever-present help in developing many of the ideas I've drawn upon for this book. I have tried to credit people for their ideas, but there is a less visible and obvious influence wider than one creditable person. Particular thanks go to the following members of the team: Emma Worley, Steve Hoggins, Andy Day, Steven Campbell-Harris, Joe Tyler and Andy West.

Outside of The Philosophy Foundation, thanks go to Jason Buckley and Tom Bigglestone of thephilosophyman.com for offering ideas and comments on my ideas, Roger Sutcliffe of DialogueWorks for looking over the philosophy section for me, and Pieter Mostert for many stimulating conversations around the topic of questioning but also for providing me with some ideas to put in the book (I have noted Pieter's contributions that were offered in conversation) and for pointing me to the wonderful essay on the Trivium by Dorothy Sayers. Thanks to Catherine McCall of Epic International for many related conversations and for being a general inspiration. I would also like to thank Laura D'Olimpio, Andrew Peterson and Michael Hand of *The Journal of Philosophy in Schools* who accepted and edited the papers that led to the further development of some of the core ideas in this book, particularly open questioning mindset (OQM) and ideas related to open and closed questions and metacognition; and thanks to Félix García Moriyón of ICPIC for editing a paper that helped me to develop ideas on teaching critical thinking.

Finally, I must include my daughter Katie for keeping me grounded: 'Daddy, stop asking me questions and just read the story!'

This book is dedicated to my friend and questioner extraordinaire Pieter Mostert.

Introduction

'Posing questions is the central act of reading the world: it must become a habit.' (Eric Booth, *The Everyday Work of Art*)

As a teacher you question constantly, maybe a hundred times a day, hundreds of times a week, thousands of times a month. Questioning is the basic tool of the teacher and so, like the butcher's knife, it should be sharp, efficient and wisely used. However useful a knowledge of question types is, it is not enough for *good* questioning.

The 'key ideas' in this book draw your attention to those more general principles that run through this book, pulling together the 100 ideas into a unified whole and creating a question-centred pedagogy rather than an arbitrary list of questioning tools. By 'question-centred pedagogy' I mean to advocate – like Socrates in Plato's *Meno* (see Idea 50) – the use of questions, not merely as a way of finding things out or for testing children, but to activate them as intellectual agents encountering the world. They will hopefully transform the world into possibilities rather than seeing it as a fixed object they bump into. With the implementation of central ideas such as: an open questioning mindset (Idea 18); the community of inquiry (Idea 31); and if-ing (Idea 43), anchoring (Idea 37) and opening up (Idea 41), questioning begins not merely a dialogue between teacher and pupils, but between the class (both teacher *and* pupils) and the world.

My experience is as a facilitator and trainer of philosophical conversations in schools and, although my examples will sometimes reflect this experience, most *if not all* the principles and strategies in this book are transferable and have application across the curriculum. You will notice that I advocate the use of closed questions – rehabilitating the closed question for general use – and my closed question strategies (notably if-ing, anchoring and opening up) lend themselves to the logic-based questioning in maths, for example, as well as the open-ended discussions of philosophy, PSHE, and so on. Interestingly, the approach to questioning you will find in this book, though largely developed through my practice as a facilitator of philosophy, was begun when I was a music teacher.

Open questioning mindset (OQM)
I would say that the *keystone idea* in this book is making sure that you have the right mindset when questioning. Asking open questions, for

instance, is no good if you still maintain a closed questioning mindset (where you are looking for specific answers that you have in mind or are heavily leading the class without transparency towards a particular answer or outcome). Conversely, asking leading questions can be very fruitful if you do so with an open questioning mindset (being open to problems, alternative positions and unexpected responses). That is not to suggest that you must always be teaching as 'openly' as possible, of course; teachers have tests to teach to and aims and objectives to reach, whatever one's views are about these. I hope that you will begin to see how we can maintain an open questioning mindset in our questioning even though we may be working to a *closed agenda* (meeting certain aims and objectives in certain time constraints). These are not incompatible.

Questioning and 'questioning'

There are two important ways to think of questioning that I have drawn upon in this book, which are based upon work by J. T. Dillon (1994): 'asking questions' and 'putting something *into question*'. The first is straightforward: when thinking about questioning one needs to think about *what* questions to ask and *how* to ask them. However, the second meaning is more subtle: it's about cultivating a 'questioning classroom', about developing a questioning mindset rather than becoming overly concerned with the mechanics – important as they are – of questioning. There is, therefore, a deeper consideration in this book, which concerns looking at how questions and questioning may play a role in your teaching more generally. Questioning is an important democratic skill, so, as teachers, we should be as interested in cultivating questioners as we are in improving our own questioning.

This book aims to be as practical as possible, with the overall aim of developing good questioning mindsets in teachers and children. It is heavily cross-referenced, so you may, of course, choose to read this book from beginning to end, or you may prefer to go to what piques your interest following the many threads I've left for you to pick up and let go as you see fit. I have also shared many of my own views and experiences, but it would not be in the spirit of the book if I did not want you to question me. So, even where you don't agree with me, I hope to have sparked something in you that activates you as a reflective questioner.

A word of caution: this book is necessarily brief with each idea, so you would do well not always to rely on the book alone to get a full grasp of the ideas presented. I have pointed you to further resources where necessary.

How to use this book

This book includes quick, easy and practical ideas for you to dip in and out of, to support you in questioning effectively in the primary classroom.

Each idea includes:

- a catchy title, easy to refer to and share with your colleagues
- an interesting quote linked to the idea
- a summary of the idea in bold, making it easy to flick through the book and identify an idea you want to use at a glance
- a step-by-step guide to implementing the idea.

'Key ideas' draw your attention to the most essential ideas in the book and the question-centred pedagogy it aims to create.

Each idea also includes one or more of the following:

Teaching tip

Practical tips and advice for how and how not to run the activity or put the idea into practice.

Taking it further

Ideas and advice for how to extend the idea or develop it further.

Bonus idea ★

There are 15 bonus ideas in this book that are extra-exciting, extra-original and extra-interesting.

Share how you use these ideas and find out what other practitioners have done using **#100ideas**.

Question types and structures

Part 1

What is a question?

'In questioning...I...open up possibilities.' (Matthew Bowker)

'What is a question?' is a *good* question. And by 'good question' I mean that it is not as straightforward as one might think.

Morgan and Saxton (2006) helpfully divide questions into three types:

1 Questions that elicit information, e.g. 'What is the capital of France?'
2 Questions that shape understanding, e.g. 'What makes a city a capital city?'
3 Questions that press for reflection, e.g. 'Are capital cities necessary?'

But what do questions *do*? Questions ask something of someone and they are usually signified, grammatically, by the presence of a question mark at the end – or, in speech, with a raised inflexion at the end of a sentence to imply an expected response. One hears pre-speech children 'ask a question' by imitating the tone and inflexion of question-asking from their parents.

'To be, or not to be: that is the question' is a question with no question mark. So, in what way is this a question? It requires us to *consider*, to *wonder*, to follow what may or may not be *implied* or *entailed* by a thought. Rather than *asking* a question, Hamlet has invited himself (and his audience!) to put something *into question* (see Idea 72). However, as question expert Pieter Mostert has pointed out, many questions are nothing more than a *request*; a request being a more polite form of command. I could say, 'Give me that!', or I could ask, 'Would you mind giving that to me?' The intention is imperative, not questioning; the question is used to make it polite.

Task questions

'What was the question again?' (A million forgetful young souls...)

A task question is an explicit question you ask to the class where the task is to try to answer it, such as, 'How many squares are there on a chess board?'

Task questions should be simple and clear, even if answering them is not always straightforward. If there is an aspect to the question that is vague or unclear, it should be so deliberately. For instance, in the question above, it has not been stated whether the squares are 1-by-1 squares or others (such as 2-by-2 or 3-by-3 squares). If you expect them simply to count the 1-by-1 squares then make this clear in your question.

However, perhaps you want this to be kept vague. In which case make use of 'if-ing' strategies (see Idea 43) to explore the possibilities left open by any vagueness. For example, if someone asks, 'Does it mean 1-by-1 squares, or any squares?' you could answer using *either-or-the-if* (see Idea 44): 'If it means 1-by-1 squares, then how many squares are there on a chessboard?' and then later: 'And if it means *any* squares, then how many squares are there on a chessboard?'

It is often helpful to make task questions *thesis questions* (see Idea 3) so that positions and arguments may be elicited. An emergent (Idea 5) or nested question (Idea 4) may become a task question if a) made explicit and b) sufficiently central or important to be a main task.

Teaching tip

It is a good idea to write up task questions on the board so they are made explicit, and can be easily seen and easily remembered.

Taking it further

See also Idea 100 ('Metacognitive questions') to help children assess whether they have answered the task question, or how they can better answer it.

Thesis questions

'You don't need to say, "I think"; if you're saying it, you obviously think it!' (Teacher to pupils)

Thesis questions are a form of closed question, certainly grammatically closed, though not always conceptually closed (Idea 16). By virtue of being closed they offer the opportunity for the pupils to make judgements (Idea 24) or 'take a position', usually beginning with the prefix 'I think...'.

Teaching tip

Remember, with thesis questions, to anchor (Idea 37), then open up (Idea 41) or, with some responses, to if (Idea 43), anchor, then open up. See also 'The Question X' (Idea 17).

Taking it further

You could frame a thesis question as a 'hypothesis question' where a statement in hypothesis form is written up and the pupils have to argue for the truth or falsity of the hypothesis (see 'The Hypothesis Box' in *40 Lessons to Get Children Thinking*; Worley, 2015a).

Bonus idea ★

Jason Buckley (aka www.thephilosophyman. com) has some nice ideas for having pupils 'take a position' in his pocket book *Thinkers' Games* (2012).

Examples of thesis questions are: 'Should the Greeks have gone to war against the Trojans?', 'Is the number we are looking for odd or even?' Of course, someone may decide not to answer definitively, therefore not taking a position: 'I don't know', 'I'm in the middle', 'Maybe both', and so on (see Idea 67 for ways to take these responses further). However, these kinds of question do lend themselves to taking a position and so are good to use if that's what you want to encourage.

Thesis questions, by virtue of being closed, have the benefit of being focused and therefore 'on-track', eliciting arguments (see Idea 46) and bringing substance to discussions. They also elicit one-word or short-phrase answers. Although this can be great for encouraging intuitive responses (see Idea 53), it can result in the discussion drying up. However, this problem is easily overcome as long as you remember to open up (see Idea 41).

Thesis questions make good task questions (Idea 2).

Nested questions

'The problem with questions is that they often lead to more questions.' (Eight-year-old girl)

Nested questions are the implicit questions that lie 'nested' within or behind an explicit question.

If the question is, 'Is a starfish a fish?' then the nested questions would include, 'What is a fish?', 'What is a starfish?', 'Can something that has 'fish' in the name not be a fish?', 'How do we classify sea animals?', and so on.

Nested questions can follow from the question (such as in the examples above) or they can be a 'meta question'; a question about the question itself, for example: 'Does the question make sense?', 'Is it answerable?', 'Is it the right question?' (see Idea 100).

Questions within questions

Take a 'philosophy' question such as, 'Can you drink the water?' generated by children in response to the stimulus of a half-filled glass of water. This doesn't appear to be very philosophical but unpacking some of the possible nested questions helps us see where any philosophy might lie. One reading of 'can' gives, 'Is one *able* to drink the water?'; another gives, 'Does one have *permission* to drink the water?'; and another gives, 'Does one have a *right* to drink the water?' These nested questions lead to further questions, such as, 'Does water ever belong to anyone?'

Teaching tip

Whenever you prepare a task question for the class, make a sequential (see Idea 74) list underneath of all the nested questions related to it, and very often your lesson plan will come out of them.

Taking it further

Challenge children to unpack a question by finding more questions connected to the first. How many can they find?

Emergent questions

'Sometimes the best questions are unplanned.'

Emergent questions are the questions that emerge from pupils during a discussion, naturally and organically.

Emergent questions overlap with nested questions (Idea 4) in that emergent questions are often implicit questions that are then made explicit by being brought out during a discussion, either directly or indirectly.

Explicit emergent questions arise when a group or class member explicitly asks a question that can then be answered by the teacher or put to the group, depending on the situation. For example, if the task question (Idea 2) is: 'How many rivers are there in this photograph?', someone may ask, 'What exactly *is* a river?' This emergent question has identified one of the key nested questions that lie behind the task question. You may choose to write this new question up on the board.

Implicit emergent questions may arise if another child says, 'I don't know because that one looks more like a stream.' In this case, although the question 'What exactly is a river?' has not been asked, it has arisen from the puzzlement expressed by the pupil. The task question asked by the teacher or book has been problematised (Idea 26) and the issue of what a river is has been put 'into question' (Idea 25). One way to deal with this is to simply see how the class responds to the problematisation, and another is to make the implicit question explicit: 'Ah! That's a good question! So, [to the whole class] what exactly *is* a river?'

Hermeneutic (interpretation) questions

'...And I will never tell lies, though I cannot promise always to tell the whole truth.' (Hermes to Zeus)

This is a somewhat intimidating-sounding name, but don't be put off this otherwise very helpful question type. I have borrowed it from David Birch, author of *Provocations: Philosophy for Secondary Schools* (2014).

The word 'hermeneutic' is thought to refer to the Greek god Hermes (and if it doesn't it should!). Hermes was the messenger of the gods, moving between the divine and the human realms. People had to interpret the words of the gods and so Hermes is a fitting emblem for anything to do with the slippery and elusive notion of interpretation.

A hermeneutic question is one that asks pupils to 'unpack' meaning. So, rather than asking them if they *agree* with a statement or position, they are asked to say what they think is *meant* by the statement or position. For example, if working on Shakespeare, one would need to first ask what Hamlet means by his statement, 'for there is nothing either good or bad, but thinking makes it so' before asking pupils if they agree (with Hamlet). See also discussion around the dictum 'know thyself' (Idea 40) and 'Questioning for interpretation' (Idea 70).

Teaching tip

Sometimes this strategy of 'unpacking' a question is useful as a prelude to a main task question – and sometimes it is necessary.

Taking it further

This procedure works very well with poetry:

1 Read the poem (maybe twice!).
2 Ask, 'Are there any words or phrases you don't understand?'
3 If so, ask a hermeneutical question: 'So, what do you think this word/phrase means?'
4 Provide a context: read the relevant section and ask question 3 again.
5 Take suggestions and clarify/correct as necessary.
6 Repeat 2–5 with other words/phrases.
7 Read the poem again.
8 Ask a broader question: 'What do you think the poem means?'

Start questions, set questions and research questions

'A good lesson often starts and ends with questions.'

These three question types have a useful role to play in beginning and ending discussions.

Start questions are questions that have been asked to begin a discussion. They will not necessarily be the central focus of the discussion and are distinguished from task or thesis questions by having no dialectical properties: they do not elicit arguments and so are not a question that you would anchor to (Idea 37), for instance. They are often more anecdotal or feeling-orientated. Here is an example of a start question contrasted with a task/thesis question:

Start question: What do you think of the speech? (Open question)

Task (thesis) question: Do you agree with X when he/she said...? (Grammatically closed question)

Set questions are questions that it is good to leave the class with at the close of a discussion. They are usually asked to get pupils to ponder. However, you may choose to treat them more systematically, such as by writing them up in the question corner/wall, putting them in a question box (see Idea 99) or on an intranet discussion forum, setting them as written work, and so on.

Research questions are empirical questions (Idea 8) that come up during discussions, the facts of which are unknown to the class (and possibly to the teacher, too). They should be noted so that the class (or certain children) can be asked to research them after or during the discussion.

Empirical (factual) questions

'Miss, is it the kind of question that has an answer?'

Empirical questions ask the children to say how things are. Empirical questions can be answered by checking — in principle, anyway. Here are some different kinds of empirical question.

• **How many chairs are there in the room?**
This can be verified by direct experience and can also be co-verified by the other class members.

• **How many planets are there in the solar system?**
This is *descriptive* in that it describes the number of a certain type of body in the solar system, and *stipulative* in that what falls under the category 'planet' may change according to definitions of 'planet'.

• **Is the Earth flat?**
This can only be verified by indirect experience (seen from pictures others have taken) or inferred (the moon and other planets appear to be spherical so it's reasonable to assume that the Earth is, too).

• **Are swans white?**
This is an example of a question that was thought to be 'settled' until the discovery of black swans in 1697. After this date the answer to this question was different, even though there had always been black swans (see Idea 11).

• **Do aliens exist?**
This is an example of an open empirical question: one that one day may be settled. This question can only be answered in the affirmative, though, otherwise the question will remain an open question: if they do not exist, that is very unlikely to be settled by us.

Teaching tip

Remain open to the possible ways in which 'factual questions' may be problematisable (see Idea 26); don't take 'facts' for granted.

Taking it further

Adapt the question quadrant (Idea 97) so that pupils can sort 'factual questions' into different types.

Dichotomous and multiple-choice questions

'Would you like to be eaten first or second?' (Troll under the bridge)

Dichotomous, 'branching' and multiple-choice questions are questions with two (or more) horns, A or B. They are leading questions, but, depending on how they are used, they aren't always bad. Dichotomous and multiple-choice questions might, in fact, be very useful in the following situations.

- **With the very young**
If you read a book like *The Three Robbers* by Tomi Ungerer (2009) to a class of four- and five-year-olds and ask, 'Were the Robbers good men?', they are likely to answer, 'Yes' because the book ends with the robbers' good deeds. Putting the question dichotomously brings to their attention other options.
- **To encourage children to challenge dichotomies**
It is *leading* to suggest that there is only a set number of options. However, whether this is desirable depends on your questioning mindset (Idea 18): if you pose the question dichotomously *because you think there are (or WANT there to be) only two options*, this would be leading in the wrong way. However, if you remain open to further possibilities, then dichotomous questions can encourage children to challenge and 'dissolve' dichotomies.
- **For a precise agenda**
As with dichotomous questions, multiple-choice questions set a precise agenda (as with assessment questions) or they can suggest things pupils might not think of themselves. These can be useful as 'back up', especially if children don't anticipate all the possibilities, so don't lay out the multiple choices until they have outlined their own possibilities first. (See also Idea 60.)

Conceptual question structures

'What's the concept behind concept?'

Concepts are the ideas that lie behind the words that we use; the ideas that the words represent.

Here are some common concept-based question structures, which you should find helpful for planning your questioning:

1 **Noun concept-question structures**
- **What is X?** A concrete noun example is: 'What is a carrot?' An abstract noun example is: 'What is freedom?' (With abstract nouns these are also known as Socratic questions.)
- **What is not X?/What is X not?** e.g. 'What is not human?' (answer: 'An alien is not human.') or: 'What is a human not?' (answer: 'A human is not immortal.')
- **Are there different kinds of X?** e.g. 'Are there different kinds of lie?' See Idea 67.

2 **Relational concept-question structures**
- **How is X different/similar to Y?/Are X and Y the same?** e.g. 'How is steam different from ice?' or 'Is water the same as ice?'
- **What is X's relationship to Y?** e.g. 'How are freedom and choice related?'
   ° **Can you have X and Y?** e.g. 'Can you be both just and kind?'

3 **Verb concept-question structures**
- **What is it to (do) X?** e.g. 'What is it to win?'
- **What is it to be X?** e.g. 'What is it to be kind?'
- **What is X-ing?** e.g. 'What is thinking?'

4 **Verb and noun-concept structure**
- **Can you V (verb) N (noun)?** e.g. 'Can you have freedom?' 'Is it possible to break water?' (Thanks to David Birch for this question.)

Knowledge questions

'But, how do you *really know* that you know?'

Episteme is ancient Greek for 'knowledge', so epistemological questions are questions to do with knowledge. Epistemology might seem obscure but it is, as the think-tank Demos have said in a report, at the heart of a problem of digital literacy with children today (Bartlett and Miller, 2011). *What* we know and *how* we know is really current with buzzwords like 'fake news', 'alt facts', 'fact-check' and 'post-truth'.

Understood in the most straightforward way, knowledge questions are questions we ask to *test* knowledge ('What is the capital of France?' Answer: 'Paris.'). However, one may not just want to test *what* one knows, one may want to ask *how* one knows ('How do you know that Paris is the capital of France?' Possible answer: 'I looked it up in an atlas.') The third level is a *reflective* question, '*How do you know that you know X?*' where the answer will be a more sophisticated explanation that might include considering any problems involved (see Idea 26), such as whether the atlas is out of date, and highlighting the stipulative, contingent nature of some facts (i.e. they are not necessarily fixed forever – see Idea 8).

Here are simple questions to illustrate the three levels:

- **Testing** for knowledge: 'What is the answer to the sum 2 + 2?'
- **Explaining** knowledge: 'How did you work that out/know?'
- **Reflecting** on knowledge: 'How do you know if that's right?'

The third level of depth here takes a question from merely a *question one is asking* to putting an issue *into question* (see Idea 25).

Ethical questions

'I could of. I would of. But *should* I of?' (Ten-year-old)

Ethical questions are questions where you ask the children to say something about how things (or how *they think* things) *should* or *ought* to be.

Ethical or moral questions will usually contain certain key words such as *ought, should, right/ wrong, acceptable, okay*, and sometimes, *have to* or *must*. Although these words are used to make moral or ethical claims, they have other functions too, such as non-moral necessity or likelihood, e.g. 'It *should* remain sunny today.'

Some common ethical-question structures are:

Surface level

- Is it okay/acceptable/right to X?
- Should F do X?

Seeking counter-examples (see Idea 71)

- When would it not be okay to X?/When would it be okay to X?

Sometimes, in response to an ethical question, pupils avoid the ethical demand of the question (the 'ought') by providing a descriptive answer (an 'is'): 'Is it okay to hit someone back if they hit you?', 'Most people would hit back!' In that case, you can anchor them to the ethical dimension by 'oughting' them: 'So, "most people would hit back" [quoting verbatim]; do you think that they *should* hit back?'

Taking it further

To go deeper with ethical questions, use the following structures:

- What makes it okay to do X?
- Is it ever/never okay to X?
- Is it always wrong to X?
- Is it sometimes okay/ wrong to X? (See Idea 51)
- *How should we decide* whether it's okay to do X? (Important for ethical decision- making processes and principles)

(See also Idea 90.)

Interrogative questions

'*Interrogate* is from the Latin *interrogat* (questioned) [and derives from] the verb *interrogare*, from *inter* (between) and *rogare* (ask).' (Oxford Dictionary of English)

The word 'interrogation' can evoke unpleasant associations. However, sometimes the act of questioning itself is described as an interrogative process.

Putting to one side for now whether all questioning is interrogative, probing can be essential to help go deeper, so this kind of questioning does have its place. However, there are some important considerations to bear in mind.

Opening up
Sometimes, asking interrogative or probing questions is no more than opening up (see Idea 41) successively: 'Can you say why?' then 'Can you give an example?'

Devil's advocate
With qualifications, there is a place for this move (see Ideas 58 and 65). However, I would advise considering other ways to achieve the same ends.

Mindset
To ensure that you are probing *in the right way*, keep an eye on your mindset (see Idea 18). If someone is experiencing discomfort from interrogative questions, it is probably because of the wrong mindset in the questioner.

Body language
Keep an eye on your body language, eye contact and tone when questioning in this way. You can minimise any negative effects by getting this right.

Trust
You will be able to get the benefits of interrogative/probing questions if there is trust in your classroom (see Idea 19).

Leading (and loaded) questions

'What is a leading question? Could it be a question that answers itself?'

A leading question contains a suggestion or assumption within it as to what the answer could be. There are two kinds: rhetorical (when the teacher hopes to get a certain answer) and inferential (when the teacher wants to know what the pupil thinks might follow). The latter, provided the mindset is right, can be a virtue.

Examples of leading questions would be, 'How are you enjoying your meal?', or 'Do you think that smoking should be made illegal or do you think people should be free to kill themselves?' The first leads by assuming you *are* enjoying your meal, drawing your attention to *how* rather than *whether* you do; the second leads by proposing answers dichotomously, A or B (Idea 9), then hinting at 'the right one'. The second is also a loaded question: a question that appeals to one's emotions to strongly suggest an answer.

One can lead with more than just a question: tone, body language and facial expression. Here are some ways that leading questions can be useful:

- **Atomic anchoring:** anchoring to more than one part of a question to make sure the answer addresses both parts (Idea 39).
- **Possibling:** asking someone to stretch their thinking to consider whether something is possible, e.g. pupil: 'Humans are basically selfish'; teacher: 'Is it *possible* that a human can do something that is not selfish?'
- **Dichotomous questioning and multiple choice:** setting out and limiting the options in the question (Idea 9).

Teaching tip

To use leading questions effectively, keep an eye on your questioning mindset (Idea 18). For example, *possibling* could be used to lead in a bad way ('I want you to come to conclusion X!') or a good way ('I want to know what you think.')

Taking it further

Watch a courtroom drama to see how leading questions are used by lawyers to achieve their own goals. Also look out for dichotomies – often false ones! (See Idea 9.)

Implicit open questions, explicit closed questions

'This is a question.'

Open-ended questions, such as 'What is X?', are the basis for exploratory discussions, although they are not always the best questions to ask. However, even if you choose to use other question types, don't lose sight of the implicit open questions lurking in the background.

If you want to explore the nature of numbers with your class, instead of simply asking the broad, dry and abstract question, 'What is a number?', use a grammatically closed question (Idea 16), such as, 'Is zero a number?' Notice that, in contrast to the open question, it is narrower, concrete and less dry. However, the implicit, conceptually open questions within it are: 'What is a number?' and 'What is zero?', so it will still help you to fulfil your objective of exploring the nature of numbers. Opening-up is one way to access these implicit open issues: 'So, why is zero not a number?' or 'If it's not a number then what is a number?', etc. (See Ideas 4 and 41.)

Imagine that you want to discuss poetry with your class. You could start by asking the open question, 'What is poetry?' or the following explicit closed question (containing the implicit open question):

Is

This

A

Poem?   (Taken from *40 Lessons to Get Children Thinking*; Worley, 2015a)

(The implicit open question is: 'What is poetry?')

Key idea: Open and closed questions

'Really interesting distinction between "grammatically" and "conceptually" open and closed questions.' (Twitter user)

It is far from clear exactly what an open or closed question is, and as a result we don't often know how to fully utilise them effectively. This idea offers a useful distinction.

'A closed-ended question [...] can be answered with a simple "yes" or "no", or with a specific piece of information. An open-ended question cannot be answered with a "yes" or "no", or with a static response.' (Wikipedia) So, are the following open or closed questions?

1 What is the answer to the sum 2 + 2?
2 What is the mind?
3 What facts can you tell me about Paris?
4 Is the mind the same as the brain?

The first two are fairly straightforward on the usual understanding: 1 is closed and 2 is open. It is 3 and 4 that tend to divide opinion. The distinction lies between *grammatical* and *conceptual* open and closed questions. A *grammatically* open or closed question is open or closed by virtue of its *structure*. A *conceptually* open or closed question is open or closed by virtue of the *concepts* (ideas, meaning, relationships) involved. Here are the above questions with the new distinction in place:

Teaching tip

So, not only is it good to use both open and closed questions, you can *combine* open and closed questions (see also Idea 17).

Taking it further

Read the article 'Open thinking, closed questioning: two kinds of open and closed question' published in the *Journal of Philosophy in Schools*, available online (Worley, 2015b; open access).

	Grammatically open	Grammatically closed
Conceptually open	'What is the mind?'	'Is the mind the same as the brain?'
Conceptually closed	'What facts...?'	'What is the answer to the sum 2 + 2?'

Key idea: The Question X

'A really useful, practical strategy that I will use tomorrow.' (Teacher)

This is a staple in any teacher's questioning repertoire that has a really important role to play in eliciting substantive ideas that can be *evaluated* (see Idea 46) with the use of closed questions (Idea 16).

Closed questions can be visually represented like this: > This shape captures what is both good and bad about closed questions. What's good is that they are extremely *focused* and specific; what's bad is that they have a tendency to *close down* discussions by producing short responses such as, 'Yes', 'No', 'Maybe', 'It depends' or 'I dunno!'

Open questions can be represented like this: < This also captures what is both good and bad about open questions. What's good is that they *invite* one to say what one wants to and they are *indeterminate* (they are often not looking for one specific answer). What's bad is that they can 'go anywhere' and are consequently very difficult to keep under control. This is what often leads discussions based around open questions alone to veer off-track very easily. So, my recommendation is to combine the approaches into the Question X:

Ask a closed question.	X	Then open it up!
e.g. 'Should the Greeks go to war?'	'No.'	'Why not?'

The Question X gives you the best of both worlds: the *focus* of a closed question, but also the *eliciting* quality of open questions. Discussions stay on-track but they don't dry up.

There is also a deeper reason why the Question X is so useful – it's a strategy that helps pupils to both *think* and *answer* in a way that produces *arguments*, i.e. a conclusion supported by reasons (see Idea 46).

Developing a questioning classroom

Part 2

Key idea: Questioning mindsets

'...for I, myself, don't really know yet, but whatever direction the argument blows us, that's where we must go.' (Socrates in *Republic*)

Asking the right question can be important, but more important is the questioning mindset you are in.

A **closed questioning mindset** (CQM) is when the questioner has a preconceived expectation of what answer they are looking for (e.g. 'What is the capital of France?'), or what they think the questionee is thinking (e.g. 'So, what you mean is...').

An **open questioning mindset** (OQM) is when the questioner expects the pupil to only report *what they think* and *why they think it* rather than *what they think the questioner wants them to say* (mind-reading).

Key features of the two mindsets are:

Open questioning mindset	Closed questioning mindset
1 Listening out for *what* the child thinks/says.	1 Listening for *what you want* the child to think/say.
2 Listening out for *why* the child thinks what they think or said what they said.	2 Not listening for this!
3 Being open to problematisation and alternative possibilities (Idea 26).	3 Avoiding or *blocking* (Idea 40) problematisation and alternative possibilities.
4 Listening out for the need for more from the child (e.g. further clarification and explanation).	4 Not listening out for these!
5 Always on the lookout for the possible limits of the teacher's own knowledge or understanding.	5 Tending to see themselves as right or in possession of correct knowledge.
6 Always on the lookout for learning opportunities.	6 Not on the lookout for learning opportunities!

One can have an open or closed questioning mindset whether one is using open or closed questions. See below:

1 A CQM with a closed question:
Teacher: What is the answer to the sum 2 + 2?
Pupil 1: Is it 22?
Teacher: No. Anyone else?
Pupil 2: Is it 4?
Teacher: Yes, well done!

2 An OQM with a closed question:
Teacher: What is the answer to the sum 2 + 2?
Pupil 1: Is it 22?
Teacher: Could you say why you think it is 22?
Pupil 1: Because if you take a '2' and add it to another '2' you get '22'.
The teacher then determines to teach the difference between digits and values and the difference between '+' as conjunction and '+' as arithmetical operation.

3 A CQM with an open question:
Teacher: What is poetry?
Pupil 1: It's boring!
Teacher: [*Ignoring P1*] Anyone else?
Pupil 2: It rhymes.
Teacher: Well done! [*Writes 'rhyme' up on the board*]

4 An OQM with an open question:
Teacher: What is poetry?
Pupil 1: It's boring!
Teacher: Can you say why you think it's boring?
Pupil 1: Coz it's got like 'ye olde' words.
Teacher: Has anyone something to say about that? Yes...?
Pupil 2: Not all poetry has old words. Rap isn't boring and it doesn't have old words.
Pupil 1: But rap's not poetry.
Pupil 2: Yes, it is. It rhymes, it has rhythm, it expresses feelings and ideas.
Teacher: [*To everyone*] So, is rap poetry?

Teaching tip

In the fourth example, the teacher allows for problematisation, invites responses from anyone, allows a controversy to emerge and to 'bite' with the class so that it matters to them and, finally, uses the emergent question, 'Is rap poetry?' to be the focus rather than the more abstract, 'What is poetry?' (see Idea 15).

Taking it further

For more on this see my paper 'Ariadne's Clew: absence and presence in the facilitation of philosophical conversations' in *Journal of Philosophy in Schools* (Worley, 2016a), available online and with open access.

Key idea: Cultivating trust and accountability

'Trust is built when someone is vulnerable and not taken advantage of.' (Bob Vanourek)

If asked a question, children need to feel that they won't be made to feel or look foolish. There are four main points to remember.

1 Listen actively.

Active listening involves much more than hearing what is being said (see Idea 21).

2 Invite.

Invite all to contribute, and remember: someone who is *invited* to do something should always be able to exercise their right to decline.

3 Ensure appropriate accountability.

Respond to errors appropriately: *consistently* so that they can predict how you will respond, and *fairly*, while promoting their intellectual agency. Give the information needed for correction and if something contestable is said, invite others to engage with them appropriately and respectfully, providing reasons for their responses.

4 Right-to-reply and proper consideration.

If someone does critically engage with someone else's idea, allow them to exercise their right to reply. They may add a qualification, revise their original idea or change their mind. Sometimes your role will be to ensure that the children fulfil their responsibility for proper consideration, because children do sometimes ignore important objections to their ideas. Gently hold them to this: 'So, how do you respond to F's idea that...?'

Approval

'Should we approve of approval?' (Teacher in training)

When pupils respond to questions, should you offer approval of their contribution? This issue deserves some careful consideration.

Clearly, we want to encourage our pupils when they respond to questions, but we may do more damage than we intend by doing this too much or too strongly. We might think we are building self-esteem by saying 'positive' things about contributions. However, if they are *unwarranted* 'positives', we may be undermining pupils' self-esteem in the long term, not building it.

One problem with approval responses is that they can *close down diversity*: once the children hear that a certain response is 'approved' they will often say the same or a very similar thing, thinking that's what the teacher is looking for.

It is better to encourage with attentive listening (Idea 21) and positive body language rather than through approval words like 'Good job!' or 'Fantastic!'. You may, of course, mean, 'It's fantastic that you've said something!' but you may be *heard* to mean, 'Fantastic answer! That's what I'm looking for!'

When you *do* praise, do so carefully and deliberately and make sure that the praise is warranted. For instance, if someone demonstrates a good example of the kind of thinking that is called for during a particular activity (e.g. they use a counter-example, see Idea 71), highlight this. Also, when praising be transparent and say exactly *what* you are praising and *why*. On the whole, it is better to be sparing with praise and approval.

Teaching tip

Find a fairly neutral default response to pupils, such as 'Interesting' or 'Thank you!' but bear in mind that even these, with the wrong tone, can be far from neutral.

Taking it further

See Idea 48 ('Descriptive teaching') for more ways to highlight praise-worthy responses and behaviour by your pupils.

Bonus idea ★

Carol Craig has written and researched around self-esteem and wellbeing, challenging many preconceptions: http://www.centreforconfidence.co.uk/usingthesite.php.

Listening

'The art of listening [is] a polyphonic activity.' (Pablo Muruzábal Lamberti, 'Apprentices of listening', The Philosophy Foundation blog)

One of the most important intellectual virtues is sensitivity (see Idea 23). Good questioning (from teacher or pupil) must be informed by intellectual sensitivity, and this is achieved through good listening.

Teaching tip

Be transparent and honest! Don't pretend to have been listening when you have not been. There are so many distractions and interruptions in a classroom so it is fine to be honest about this. Simply apologise for not hearing them and ask the pupil to repeat what they said.

Taking it further

Read this article about listening in philosophy, which should be useful to anyone interested in improving their active listening: 'Apprentices of listening' by Pablo Muruzábal Lamberti (2018) on The Philosophy Foundation's blog: www. philosophy-foundation. org/blog/apprentices-of-listening.

Hearing is involuntary and passive, while listening requires effort and so is an *activity*: hearing happens to you, listening you do. So, when you listen to someone, you not only hear, but you also interpret and evaluate. As Lamberti (see 'Taking it further') says, this means that you are listening not only to the person speaking but also to your own 'inner voice'.

Listening is not just about making sure you (and the pupils) know what has been said; it is also about *considering* what has been said, ensuring that it is being considered by others and not doing anything else other than listen. (See also Idea 19.) Difficult, I know, with all the pressures and demands made on teachers minute-to-minute. But, where possible, devote your ears, your eyes and your mind to the children when they speak. True listening is where you *receive* what they say rather than *imposing* or *hoping* for something they may well not say. This requires an open questioning mindset (Idea 18). You must also do your best to ensure that the children listen to each other and that all children are listened to and with equal respect.

Aporia: being comfortable with discomfort

'You don't get confused...well, you get confused sometimes.'
(Ten-year-old on philosophy)

Aporia is an ancient Greek word that comes from the word *poros*, meaning 'path' or 'way forward'. When the prefix 'a' is added, *aporia* means 'pathlessness'.

I use *aporia* to refer to all those experiences one has that are to do with 'losing one's way': perplexity, confusion, ambiguity, uncertainty, frustration, boredom, not knowing. Very often, these experiences are seen as *bad things*.

There are (at least) two kinds of confusion: *absent* confusion and *present* confusion. Absent confusion is when one is confused or lost because one was not 'in the room', either literally (they were away, ill), or figuratively (they were not listening). Here, confusion follows from a deficit of understanding. Present confusion is when one has been listening and attempting to follow something, but then reaches difficulty. Here, confusion follows from partial understanding.

One very important attitude that a 'questioning classroom' cultivates and encourages is to embrace the *aporetic* (perplexity, confusion, etc.) Some will become 'numbed' by *aporia* and may walk away, angered. Others see it as a call to arms to search for a solution or insight. The questioning teacher aims to cultivate the second kind of psychological disposition among their pupils: children who not only seek a path when they stray from one, but who may *actively seek* to explore the undergrowth, deliberately leaving the path when they are on one.

Teaching tip

Model your celebration of the *aporetic* – make visible your own confusion, as well as your own willingness to make mistakes.

Taking it further

Why not teach this unusual word to the class and have them become 'an *aporia* class'?

Bonus idea ★

The educator James Nottingham has captured these ideas in his concept of 'the learning pit', which he has couched in terms of Dweck's growth mindset principles (Idea 49). According to Nottingham, one begins in *clarity*, then moves through *confusion* to reach '*Eureka!*' (another ancient Greek word that literally means, 'I found [it]!'). See: www.jamesnottingham.co.uk/learning-pit/.

Intellectual virtues

'A good mind, like a good knife, is sharp.'

Think of 'virtue' in this context as 'that which makes one good at something', just as a knife, in order to be a *good* knife, must be sharp. Here we are considering what makes a good pupil, or a 'knower', 'learner' and 'understander'.

I have identified five central intellectual virtues:

- Willingness
- Responsibility
- Judgement
- Evaluation
- Sensitivity

The basic requirement for questioning as a teaching tool is that those you question be **willing** to engage (see Idea 19).

Pupils need to take intellectual **responsibility** for their answers. They should be prepared to engage with those they critique, and should expect similar responsibility to be taken by their peers. As teacher, you need to provide the right conditions for responsibility and accountability (see Idea 19).

Pupils need to be prepared to make **judgements**, to know what it is to make a judgement and not to be afraid of making judgements (see Idea 24).

Likewise, pupils need to be prepared to **evaluate**, to know what it is to do so and not to be afraid of doing so (see Ideas 46, 47 and 53).

Finally, pupils need to be **sensitive** to any changes that might impact on what is needed in an intellectual situation. Asking metacognitive questions (Idea 100) is one way to activate their sensitivity to intellectual/ learning situations and any changes to them that may occur.

Judgements

'It is only shallow people who do not judge by appearances.' (Oscar Wilde)

Don't be afraid of asking children to make judgements. If you ask someone if they agree with X, they will have to make a judgement of some kind. They may think that what was claimed is not true or they may think that it needs qualification or is inconsistent and so on. These are all forms of appropriate judgement-making.

It is important not to confuse *judgement-making* with *judgementalism*. The latter is where you make a prejudiced or premature judgement, or when you 'jump to conclusions'. It's fine to discourage judgementalism in your classroom but don't throw 'judgement-making' out with it!

Just because someone states their opinion does not mean that their opinion can't be wrong or that it is in need of no justification or revision. Imagine someone were to say, 'Girls can't catch!' and when asked why they thought this they said, 'Because I saw a girl try to catch a ball yesterday and she couldn't catch it.' Even if their example were true, they would not be entitled to this general opinion because a single example does not entitle one to infer a general claim. In short, it is not a *sound inference*.

Even very young children have a natural ability to spot poor inferences. Usually, they do so using the following structure: 'Just because... does not mean that...' Listen out for any examples of the children using this structure in discussions. Then highlight it and provide them with the structure they've used ('Just because... does not mean that...') to use more strategically in future (see Idea 48).

Also see the Question X, Idea 17.

Teaching tip

Here are some questions to help elicit judgement-making:

- What do you think about that?
- Do you agree with X?
- Do you think that's right/okay/acceptable/true?

Taking it further

Learn about critical thinking skills – good rules for forming sound judgements. Try *Thinking from A to Z* by Nigel Warburton (2007).

To question or not to question: that is the question!

'The principle of teacher questioning during discussion runs: *Do not put questions to students during a discussion.*' (James T. Dillon, 1994)

Dillon goes on to say, '...instead, use alternatives to questioning. For instance, state your thought to the pupil.' This seems to go against almost everything this book stands for, so how should we respond to this claim?

Teaching tip

Yes, you should understand that 'questioning' goes beyond 'asking questions', but don't *stop* questioning altogether in discussions: question better!

Taking it further

Conduct your own research. Record yourself or a colleague using different questioning strategies and note the quantity and quality of the responses and ensuing discussion.

I have drawn upon an important distinction from Dillon in this book: that between *asking questions* and *putting things into question*, so several ideas in this book ask the teacher to approach questioning in a way that does *not* require asking questions. In Idea 72 I also recommend the occasional use of statements to put things into question. So far, so good.

However, Dillon points out that in the transcripts taken from the research the pupils say less when they are asked questions by the teacher and say more when the teacher states a thought (page 85). We should not conclude from this that we should not ask questions but that, perhaps, the questioning techniques of the teachers in the transcripts are not optimum.

Secondly, he claims that pupils say less when questioned by teachers, than when responding to thoughts from teachers. However, that may well be because the teachers are only asking closed questions and failing to open them up.

We should not conclude that *when more is said all the better*; a shorter answer may be a better answer. And by saying 'teacher thoughts', we may lose some pupil ownership, even if pupils do say more in response.

Problematisation

'A problem shared is a problem...halved? Solved? Doubled?'
(Variations on an English proverb)

A problem anticipated is a problem that's not going to trip you up later! A 'questioning classroom' is not afraid of problems.

Consider the following 'sticky' situation:

Teacher: A sentence is something that begins with a capital letter and ends with a full stop.
Child: [*Writes*] F. [*Then says*] That's not a sentence.

The pupil is *problematising*. Problematisation is the principle at work when we call something 'into question'. The cynical might call this 'problem-creating', but I prefer to call it 'problem-seeing' or 'anticipating'. Children are very good at spotting problems with something so it's in your interests to:

1 anticipate possible problems before they do;
2 be open to problems when the children *do* spot them, or *think* they've spotted them – sometimes it's a false problem in need of explanation or clarification.

There is also an important third approach to problematisation: not only to anticipate for oneself and to remain open to it, but also *to actively task the class to seek problems with something* (see Idea 22).

In order to cultivate a healthy problematising classroom:

- Maintain an open questioning mindset (Idea 18).
- Embrace the aporetic (Idea 22).
- Invite the use of critical-thinking tools, such as questioning for counter-examples (Idea 71),
- Where over-problematising is not appropriate, *say yes and stipulate as needed* (see 'Teaching tip' in Idea 5 for an example).

Teaching tip

Be in the habit of asking, after you have presented or explained something, 'Are there any problems with this?' as well as the usual, 'Does anyone not understand?'

Taking it further

Philosophy and P4C (Idea 90) is a great way to introduce the children to *systematic problematisation*, and the idea that problematising is a good thing!

Socratic irony

'In respect of knowledge, I am wise only in that I do not claim to know what I do not know.' (Socrates in Plato's *Apology* – often misquoted as, 'I only know one thing: that I know nothing.')

Sometimes it's good to take a position of 'not-knowing' to galvanise your class. Sometimes it's also important to recognise that perhaps you don't know what you thought you did!

Socrates often *appears* ignorant in order to demonstrate to his interlocutor, through questioning, that they *are* ignorant about what they think they know. The irony lies in the fact that Socrates really knows that his interlocutor is more ignorant than they think. In these cases, Socrates is in a *closed questioning mindset*. However, sometimes, particularly when with friends rather than adversaries, he seems to share in their ignorance: '...for I myself really don't know yet, but whatever direction the argument blows us, that's where we must go.' (*Republic*) In these cases, he is in an *open questioning mindset*.

From this, we see that there are two ways that we can understand Socratic irony in the classroom: pretending to be wrong or ignorant when you are not wrong or ignorant, or recognising that there is room for genuine doubt on an issue. 'Conveniently forgetting' (see 'Ellipsis' in Idea 41) a word or an idea in order to spark a response might be an appropriate use of the first position. However, maintaining an open questioning mindset helps create a culture of open enquiry in the classroom (see Idea 31). The key difference between the two is that the first is disingenuous, while the second is not.

The metacognitive teacher

'Be your own "critical friend"!' (A critical friend who was too busy!)

One frequently recommended way of evaluating your own questioning (and other things) is to invite a colleague in to observe you questioning as a 'critical friend'. However, finding colleagues with the time to do that is not easy. So, learn to 'watch yourself' just as a colleague would, and become a metacognitive teacher.

Most of us have developed questioning habits and tics without being aware of them, from inserting a disapproving-sounding 'Mmm...' after receiving an answer to a question – even when it's not meant as disapproving – to telling pupils what they are thinking, e.g., 'So, you think more people should vote.'

There are three stages to becoming a metacognitive teacher:

1 **Be aware!** Notice what you *do*, but also what you're *thinking*. And notice the things you do but should have thought about more, and those things that you *refrain* from doing. Why did you refrain?

2 **Monitor** your questioning and always ask yourself the following questions:

  • Was that needed?
  • What can I do to improve?

3 If necessary, **change** your questioning behaviour using appropriate **tools** and **strategies** (such as those in this book!).

Here's how to evaluate your questioning:

1 What was your **question** (or intervention)?
2 What was the **impact**? Confused silence? Did it elicit an argument?
3 **Evaluate:** Was the impact good or not? Why? What can you do in the future to improve your questioning in this context?

Teaching tip

Remember that evaluation is not merely description. Don't just say what you did but look for evidence of the impact and then say whether what you did was good or not based on that evidence.

Taking it further

Simply slipping into a 'self-observation' mode may be sufficient. However, to begin with you may also like to make notes after a questioning exchange or you may prefer to record sections of your teaching when you know you'll be questioning.

31

Dialectical vs. inclusion aims

'Sometimes being fair conflicts with a good discussion.'

Discussions often have two aims: a *dialectical* aim and an *inclusion* aim. The first of these is concerned with the right sequential development (are contributions connected in the right way?), and the second is to do with ensuring that all pupils are engaged and made to feel — and be — included.

Teaching tip

Transparency: When prioritising the dialectical aim, tell the class why you are doing what you are doing. For instance, if you use 'right-to-reply' they will see someone get two goes in close succession. Explain what 'right-to-reply' is and why you are using it.

Taking it further

McCall's 'community of philosophical inquiry' (2009; see Idea 31) provides a structural demand that each contribution is connected to previous contributions, so each speaker says something like, 'I agree with...when he/she/ they said...because...' Try using this structure in discussions to encourage better dialectical progress. McCall also suggests that participants use made-up names to depersonalise, helping with inclusion.

Sometimes the two aims, dialectical and inclusion, conflict and a decision is needed to prioritise. A good, overall balance between them is desirable.

By 'dialectic' I mean 'a systematic exploration and evaluation of opinions with the use of questions and conversation'. To help meet the dialectical aim, try these strategies:

- **Right-to-reply:** if B comments on or criticises A's idea, then it is good for the dialectical aim if A is given a chance to 'respond back' to B (Idea 19).
- **Response detector:** this is also a good way to encourage dialectical progress (Idea 83).
- **Seeking dissonance** (see Ideas 47 and 56).

To meet the inclusion aim, and make sure that all pupils are included and involved, the following ideas offer useful strategies: 36, 80, 82, 84 and 86.

Sometimes meeting the inclusion aim helps with the dialectical aim, too. If there are important ideas that will move the discussion on in important dialectical ways that are not being heard through the usual methods, then attending to inclusion will help reach those ideas.

Scepticism vs. cynicism

'I'm not a cynic, I'm a *realist*.' (Said on the Clapham omnibus)

Central to this book is the notion of 'putting things into question' (see Idea 25) and creating a 'questioning classroom', which is a culture rather than a question type or strategy. This will, to an extent, involve modelling: teacher-to-pupil and pupil-to-pupil and occasionally pupil-to-teacher.

Consider the following two expressions of doubt:

- 'How exactly did they come to that conclusion?'
- 'I doubt he's genuine; he's a politician!'

I would describe the first as an example of *healthy scepticism*. If you are shown a headline that makes a claim, even if it draws upon scientific research, it is a good thing to want to know more about how the research was done or on what basis the claim is being made. Crucially, in principle at least, it is something that one can investigate.

The second example has simply assumed the worst of someone. The hidden premise is, 'All politicians are not genuine', and this is certainly open to doubt, even if the healthy sceptic falls short of saying that it is false. This claim is also much more difficult to investigate.

The healthy sceptic wants to know what the world is like and questions world views before accepting them; the cynic makes assumptions about what the world is like that the healthy sceptic would challenge.

So, is 'the realist' a cynic or a sceptic? I can't make a general claim; it would depend on which of the profiles above they matched. In short, model 'not taking things for granted' but don't model 'always expecting the worst'.

Teaching tip

Try to avoid indoctrinating pupils with your world view; watch out for when you may have slipped from encouraging healthy scepticism to peddling cynicism!

Taking it further

Learn about and, where appropriate, teach and model good critical thinking skills. Critical thinking skills can make one a good 'room-for-doubt-detector', highlighting where one needs to check facts and sources. Philip Cam's *Twenty Thinking Tools* (2006) and Nigel Warburton's *Thinking from A to Z* (2007) are good critical thinking resources.

Community of inquiry (CoI)

'With great power comes great responsibility.' (Attributed to many, from Voltaire to Spiderman!)

A CoI appears to be self-explanatory: a community of people inquiring together. Considered more thoroughly, however, a CoI is a group of people who set out to inquire collaboratively, critically, creatively and considerately about empirical and/or conceptual aspects of any problematic issue.

CoI was originally conceived by pragmatist philosopher C. S. Peirce as a form of scientific investigation. It has since been embraced by educationalists, notably John Dewey and Matthew Lipman. 'Philosophy for children' (P4C – see Idea 90) is committed to this central pedagogical model; however, a teacher can embody CoI ideals without necessarily doing P4C in his or her classroom and many of its ideals are represented in the ideas in this book. Although the teacher does not necessarily hold the same status as the pupils with regard to knowledge, the teacher considers him or herself to be, at least to some extent, a *co-inquirer*. A CoI is not committed to the view that knowledge is decided democratically (a common misunderstanding), though it is considered to be an important way that democratic ideals are realised in education. As far as questioning is concerned, it offers an important forum for placing questions and questioning in education, so that pupils gain access to an important dialectical mechanism for them to be able to become active participants in a democratic society: to realise that they have a voice and that they have access to processes that give their voice power.

Transparency and ownership

'Justice is the virtue of order and exchange – equitable order and honest exchange.' (André Comte-Sponville)

Ownership is what the children need to have when answering questions. Transparency is what the teacher needs to ensure ownership prevails in the classroom.

Ownership is not necessarily having the children decide everything (such as what questions to ask), it is where the children answer questions and:

1 know *why* they are answering them;
2 *decide for themselves* what answer to give;
3 *accept responsibility* for answers they give;
4 have some kind of *synoptic view* (a sense of the whole) of the discussion or inquiry.

Transparency is what the just teacher exercises when questioning (and at other times, too) to ensure that exchanges are equitable, honest and visible. Ownership comes from transparency. Always have these aims in mind:

- Be clear about the *context* of your questioning (how does your question connect to other questions you ask?).
- Be clear about the *purpose* of your questioning (do they know why you are asking the questions you're asking?).
- Don't *assume implications have been understood* (is there anything you've taken for granted that you need to make explicit?).
- Ask them what *they* think.
- Give them the *option not to answer*.
- Except where absolutely necessary, *refrain from paraphrasing, summarising* and *signposting*, as any interpretation is likely to take them further away from their ownership of the discussion.

Teaching tip

To maximise the children's ownership, use contentless, structural questions and avoid hidden agendas. That is: be transparent and work with an open questioning mindset.

Taking it further

Listen here: https://philosophynow.org/podcasts/Primary_School_Philosophy to the difference of effect between the facilitator's questioning where the children answer his questions and know why they are answering them, and the interviewer's questioning where the children are able to answer his questions but don't know why they are answering them. Here's an interesting analysis of the session: https://andrewjtaggart.com/2011/11/.

Trivium: the lost tools of learning

'...they learn everything, except the art of learning.' (Dorothy Sayers)

Inspired by the ancient Greeks and Romans, medieval educators developed an educational model that has had a revival in recent years: Trivium.

Trivium (grammar, dialectic and rhetoric) contrasts with Quadrivium (arithmetic, geometry, astronomy and music) and together they make up the seven liberal arts: those arts that if practised properly set one free. The Quadrivium consisted of the 'subjects' thought to be important at the time; what we consider to be the important subjects today have changed and grown in number considerably since the Middle Ages. However, the 'tools of learning' that we see in the Trivium, *mastery of the rules* (grammar), *the science and art of reasoning* (dialectic or logic) and *the art of persuasion* (rhetoric), are, arguably, just as important today as they ever were, but are often, lamentably, overlooked and under-taught, to both pupils and their teachers.

One can question for all three pillars of the Trivium (see Bloom's taxonomy in Idea 54 for a structural approach for how to do so). However, developing the second pillar, dialectic (reasoned conversations), is central to your class becoming a 'questioning classroom'. Much of this book is devoted to developing these kinds of conversations, but implementation needs to be done responsibly and systematically (see, for instance, Idea 90 for methods for properly implementing philosophy and P4C), and one should not develop one pillar of the Trivium while neglecting the others.

Key idea: Presence and absence

'A good waiter tends to all your needs but should go unnoticed.'

Presence and absence are general classroom principles that bear on *how* we question but also *when* we question, as the art of questioning is as much to do with when we *don't* question as it is to do with when we *do*.

Presence is the extent to which a teacher/facilitator intervenes (e.g. asks a question, makes a suggestion, clarifies, or does an activity) in the classroom.

Absence is the extent to which a teacher/facilitator *refrains* from making an intervention in the classroom.

There are two chief ways in which a teacher understands their questioning interventions: in terms of either *content* (see also Idea 55) or *process* (where the teacher performs a structural role).

The art of teaching – and of questioning – is concerned with getting the balance right between appropriate and effective presence and appropriate and effective absence: when one 'steps in' and when one 'steps out'.

Many of the practical strategies in this book are expressions of both presence and absence. For instance, 'if-ing', 'anchoring' and 'opening up' are expressions of presence in that they are interventions – something the teacher does that impacts on what follows in the classroom. But, they are also expressions of absence in that the teacher performs a limited structural role so that they avoid providing idea-content to the discussion or exchange.

Teaching tip

If you 'step out' in terms of substantive idea-content, then you guarantee that the ideas said during the discussion are the pupils' own. The more you say, the less they own the discussion (see Idea 32).

Taking it further

Try to facilitate discussions so that an observer cannot tell what you think.

Bonus idea ★

Check out the related Taoist principle of *wu wei*, sometimes translated as 'doing without doing' or 'without effort', and the 'within opposites' notion of Yin and Yang. These concepts help to understand how to achieve the right balance between presence and absence (and not just in teaching!).

Wrong answers!

'"Wrong" has become something of a dirty word, but is it wrong to use it?'

So, you've asked a question and somebody has answered, but the answer is wrong. What do you do?

Teaching tip

Remember to open up 'right answers', too. You may get the answer '4' to the question 'What is 2 + 2?' only to hear, when you open up: 'Because 4 is my lucky number!'

Taking it further

See Idea 100 on metacognitive questions to encourage children to ask questions of themselves. This will help them assess their own progress and mark their own work.

First of all, we do not need to banish the word 'wrong'. One way to model this is to be wrong yourself. I wouldn't necessarily suggest being wrong deliberately (although there may be a place for this), but don't feel the need to 'cover up' when you *do* make a mistake. And, if pupils notice, when you didn't, this is to be celebrated! The higher-ability children will also need to get this message to encourage them to 'try things out'.

Here are two strategies to follow:

1 Always ask why they think what they think: open it up!

Maintain an open questioning mindset (Idea 18) and open up whether they are right or wrong (or neither). If you only open up or ask probing questions (see Idea 13) when they are wrong, you might inspire suspicion when you ask follow-up questions.

2 Treat answers seriously.

Sometimes children struggle to articulate a serious point – and sometimes they only mean to get a laugh – but there are times when a less serious point can have a significant and important impact on a discussion. So, if someone is making a point for no other reason than to get a laugh, then treating the point seriously and asking them to explain why, or to say more, will discourage rhetorical points and encourage intellectual responsibility (Idea 23).

How to respond to pupils: a checklist

'Break any of these rules sooner than say anything outright barbarous.' George Orwell, *Politics and the English Language*

Here is a useful checklist to point you in the right direction when it comes to responding to pupils.

Do:

- thank them (Idea 20)
- smile
- listen (Idea 21)
- wait
- open up (Idea 41)
- anchor (Idea 37) and open up (Idea 41)
- if (Idea 43), anchor (Idea 37) and open up (Idea 41)
- encourage (Idea 20)
- invite responses/challenges (Idea 19)
- link ideas (Idea 53)
- invite corrections
- refer them to the right/good sources to 'fact check' (Idea 11)
- echo answers (this is where you say back verbatim what the pupil said)
- try to say 'yes' in some way to what has been offered (Idea 80)
- encourage them to speak to each other in discussions, rather than always directing their comments to you
- take yourself out of their line of sight in discussions, to encourage them to speak to each other
- ask pupils to repeat themselves if you don't hear what they say (Idea 21)
- be comfortable with silence – don't always feel the need to fill it.

Teaching tip

Overall, know why you're asking a question and watch your questioning mindset (Idea 18).

Don't:

Taking it further

Record yourself and note your responses; observe colleagues and note theirs.

- answer rhetorically, ironically, or sarcastically (Idea 35)
- be dismissive
- make jokes at their expense or 'over their heads' (Idea 19)
- correct answers too quickly (Idea 35)
- paraphrase, summarise or signpost unless absolutely necessary (Idea 18)
- forget to open up grammatically closed questions (Ideas 16 and 41)
- block them (Ideas 40 and 61)
- make strong approval remarks (Idea 20)
- pretend you have been listening or have heard them when you haven't (Idea 21)
- give unwarranted praise (Idea 20)
- respond too often or too quickly
- be afraid of letting a pupil know they are wrong, but do so sensitively and appropriately (Idea 35)
- talk over pupils and interrupt them
- share your own opinions too often (Idea 34)
- show disappointment
- fall into questioning habits and tics (Idea 28).

Questioning strategies

Part 3

Key idea: Anchoring

'So simple: you just ask the question again!' (Teacher)

'Anchoring' is when you ask the main question again.

A very common anchoring situation is where a pupil says something in response to a question, but doesn't (or doesn't explicitly) answer the question. For example:

Question: Is it an odd number?

Response: It can be divided into two.

Anchor: So, is it an odd number?

Child: No.

When anchoring to grammatically closed questions (Idea 16) such as this, remember, when necessary, to open up (Idea 41):

Anchor: So, is it an odd number?

Child: No.

Opening up: Can you say why?

Child: Because you can't divide an odd number into two.

Sometimes it will be necessary to 'if' before anchoring:

Teacher: *If* you can divide the number into two, *then* [anchor] is it an odd number? (See Idea 43 for when to do this.)

There are a number of reasons why anchoring is useful when questioning:

- It helps to bring the children's contributions *back to the main question* (just as one would when answering a question in an exam).
- It helps to encourage *relevance*.
- It helps to keep the teacher/facilitator 'absent' (from content input; Idea 34).

Anchoring-to-prompt and intuitive responses

'Anchoring produces answers as a *reflex action*.' (Teacher)

You ask a child what they think or whether they've got anything they would like to say, and all they do is shrug their shoulders, say, 'Dunno' or shake their head.

When you get the sort of response described above, you could *insist* that they speak or you could simply *move to someone else*. But neither of these options is desirable: if you insist, they may, especially if they are shy, be less willing to contribute on future occasions, and if you simply *move on*, you will have missed out on any valuable contribution they may have. You will also not know what they think, making it difficult to assess 'where they're at'.

If you have a good question – clear, relevant and understandable (see Idea 2) – then simply anchor them back to it. For example imagine the question is, 'What's faster: a falcon or a cheetah?' You ask a child what she thinks a while after first asking the question, and she shrugs her shoulders. Simply ask the question again, 'So, what's faster: a falcon or a cheetah?' This is where a grammatically closed question is useful (see Idea 16) because, it being closed, the children can respond with a reflex *intuition* (e.g. 'A cheetah.').

If this strategy is successful, then remember to open up (see Ideas 17 and 41): 'Could you say why?' However, it doesn't matter if, at this point, they've not yet got more to say – that can come later.

Teaching tip

If you ask someone whether they would like to say something and they say, 'No', throw in a quick anchor! 99% of the time, the pupil *will* go on to say something in response to this simple questioning strategy. But don't force them: always invite.

Taking it further

Read the article 'Philosophy saved me from poverty and drugs' by Andy West in *The Guardian* (2015) on how this simple questioning strategy helps the less articulate. You can find it here: www.theguardian.com/ commentisfree/2015/ nov/19/philosophy-poverty-drugs-kids-young-people.

The double anchor and atomic anchoring

'Anchoring will be really useful in meetings, to keep everyone on track!' (Teacher)

Once anchoring (Idea 37) has been mastered, look out for opportunities to double anchor the pupils. A double anchor is when you anchor to a new question, then invite the pupils to see how what they've said might bear upon the first.

Teaching tip

Make use of the board and concept maps to help pupils keep track of ideas and arguments, especially when using deeper, more sophisticated questioning strategies such as this.

Taking it further

Use metacognitive questions to take this further (see Idea 100), such as, 'Have we answered the question today?' Then, you're asking the children not only to come back to the original question but also to assess how well they have answered it.

If you have started a discussion with the question, 'Was Henry VIII a good leader?' and later move to the following *emergent question* (Idea 5), 'What is a good leader?', first anchor to the new question currently being discussed ('What is a good leader?'). Then go on to see how what they've said helps to answer the overall question, 'Was Henry VIII a good leader?' Some questions are directly related to other questions (see Idea 4) in such a way that in order to answer one you will have to consider the other(s). This helps the pupils *make arguments to support other arguments*. Sometimes it will be necessary to anchor to more than one part of the same question. This is where **atomic anchoring** comes in.

For example, if you ask a question such as, 'Can you make a deliberate mistake?', some children will answer only one part of the question and think they have answered it all: 'Someone walks across the room and trips over deliberately.' This is clearly deliberate but (arguably) not a mistake as it was intended. In that case, you will need to break the question into its atomic parts:

1 'So, in your example, was it a *mistake*?'
2 'And, in your example, was it *deliberate*?'
Then synthesise them again:
3 'So, was it a *deliberate mistake*?'

Making connections: self-anchoring

'What's X got to do, got to do with Y?' (Abstracted, Tina Turner)

In many cases, when a group moves off-track during a discussion, anchoring (Idea 37) will be sufficient to bring the group back on track. However, sometimes anchoring doesn't work structurally because the new discussion is not related in the right dialectical way.

Once, I had told the class about the Oracle at Delphi and its inscription 'know thyself'. The question I had asked them was, 'What do you think "know thyself" means?' (a *hermeneutic* question – Idea 6). This had started wonderfully, with a genuine and sustained attempt to unpack the phrase. Then someone mentioned bullying and the discussion became about bullying. It became what seemed a very different discussion, and one where simply anchoring would be unsatisfactory as it would devalue what was an important discussion for them by ignoring it and moving back to the first task (what I call 'blocking').

The solution gave me a new strategy, one that synthesised both discussions. The question I asked was, 'What, if anything, do the two conversations you've had have to do with each other?' Not only did it bring things back on track, it also made sure that both conversations were included in what followed – not merely as a *token* inclusion gesture but meaningfully, in which the children were activated to make the connections between the two conversations. In this case, it led to a discussion about whether a bully *knows* that they are a bully (knowing thyself) and under what conditions one would be entitled to say that someone is a bully (knowing others).

Teaching tip

Very often, when it may appear that *you* have work to do (bringing the children back on track, signposting or summarising, and so on), it actually works better if you turn to *them* to do the work.

Taking it further

See also the 'Text-to-self, text-to-text, text-to-world' questioning and analysis approach for making connections between texts, the self and the world: https://sites.google.com/a/alaska.edu/diane-kardash/Home/making-connections.

Key idea: Opening up

'There was still more I wanted to say!' (Nine-year-old girl)

When you ask questions, especially closed questions, use the Question X (Idea 17) and remember to open them up — that is, have the pupil say more about their response to the question.

Explicit opening-up strategies

What one says to open up will depend on what it is the pupil has said. Here are the main *contentless* (see Idea 55) opening-up demands and corresponding strategies:

Common pupil response	Opening-up strategy
'Yes.'/'No.'	'Why?' (Opening up for *justification/ explanation/purpose/motivation* – see Idea 75)
'It depends.'	'What does it depend on?' (Opening up for *dependence*)
'They're not the same.'	'In what way/how are they different?' (Opening up for *comparison*)
'It's a *digit*, not a *number*.'	'What do you mean by "digit"/"number"?' (Opening up for *clarification*)
'Poetry is an emotion.'	'Can you say more about that?' (Opening up for *elicitation*)
'Maybe.'	'Why maybe?' (Opening up for *uncertainty* – see Idea 22)
'I don't know.'/'I don't understand.'	'Why don't you know?'/'Why don't you understand?' (Opening up for *knowledge/ understanding* – see Idea 11)
'Not all birds fly.'	'Can you give an example of a bird that doesn't fly?' (Opening up for *exemplification*)
'What if the situation were reversed?'	'Can you say what you think is important about your question?' (Opening up for *salience* or importance more than mere relevance)

Implicit opening-up strategies

Sometimes it's more appropriate to use implicit opening-up strategies, such as:

- **Ellipsis:** This is where you trail off to allow the pupil to continue. For instance, 'Because...?' or, 'What were you saying about it not being the river's fault...', and so on.
- **Key words:** 'You were saying something about whose *fault* it was...' If using this, ensure that you use *only key words the pupil has introduced*.
- **Silence/wait-time:** Simply wait for the pupil to open up for themselves.
- **Gesture/facial expression/body language:** Hand signals, a look or other physical indicators can encourage a pupil to go on.

How to open up

Take a look at the examples above and consider the difference between 'Why don't you know?' and 'Could you say why you don't know?' or 'Do you mind saying why you said, "I don't know?"' Consider also the difference in emphasis between '*Why* don't you know?' and 'Why *don't you know*?'

In the opening-up strategies above I've given you the basic structures. However, I will now suggest that you add a prefix to most of the strategies that will soften the edge of the basic structures (see also Idea 75) – something like, 'Can you...' or 'Do you mind...'. There are a number of reasons for this. Firstly, it is gentler and more inviting, and secondly, *it preserves the right of the pupil to decide for themselves whether to respond or not*. Sometimes a child is simply unable, for a variety of reasons, to articulate a response or provide a reason (see Idea 53) at a particular time, even though they may have provided an answer.

Taking it further

Sometimes you'll need to open up more than once (see Idea 13), e.g:

- **Child:** It's not always good to help people.
- **Teacher:** Could you say why not? (*Opening up for justification*)
- **Child:** Because sometimes you need to be 'cruel to be kind'.
- **Teacher:** Can you say what you mean by 'cruel to be kind'? (*Opening up for clarification*)
- **Child:** When you do something to someone they don't like because it's good for them.
- **Teacher:** Can you give an example? (*Opening up for exemplification*)

Opening up 'I don't know'

'If I don't know I don't know, I think I know. If I don't know I know, I think I don't know.' (R. D. Laing)

When children answer 'I don't know,' or with a shrug of the shoulders, it's difficult to know what to do. These responses could mean many things. It could mean that the child doesn't know the answer! But it could mean other things, too.

'I don't know' could mean (among other things)...

- 'I don't want to answer in front of others.'
- 'I can't be bothered to answer.'
- 'I don't know because I haven't understood.'
- 'I don't know because I see a problem.'

So, be careful not to give up straight away. You can always open up 'I don't know,' with 'Could you say why you don't know or are confused?'

There are two kinds of confusion/ignorance. One is 'absent' confusion and ignorance, where a pupil is either figuratively or literally absent from the class, and the other is 'present' confusion and ignorance, where the pupil is confused as a result of attempting to engage with and understand something. Sometimes this confusion reflects not a problem with them but with *what* they are being taught or *how* it's being taught (see Idea 22).

In Plato's dialogue *Meno*, Socrates questions a slave boy to solve a problem so that he can demonstrate to his companion, Meno, that it is possible to teach only with questions. One of the many insights offered in this short dialogue is a distinction between two kinds of ignorance:

1 thinking one knows when one does not know
2 recognising that one does not know (see Idea 27). This approach encourages the pupils to reflect on their 'I don't know!'.

Key idea: If-ing

'When the children answer with "Maybe...", then *they're* if-ing *you*.'

This central inference-making strategy makes use of the conditional form (if...then...), and constitutes one part of the three-in-one strategy 'if-ing, anchoring and opening up'.

'If-ing' is where you take what has been said by the pupil and test it against the question that is being considered. So, if your question is, 'Is it an even number?' and they say, 'It can't be divided by two,' you could 'if' this thus: 'If it can't be divided by two, then is it an even number?' Once they answer, you'll sometimes need to open up (see Idea 41).

'If-ing' for inferencing

You might think that anchoring and opening up are enough. So, with the above example, you could simply have anchored: 'So, is it an even number?' However, sometimes pupils take this as a *different* question and not as a continuation of the first. This is especially likely with younger children. 'If-ing' helps to keep them on-track, ensuring that the pupils make an inference based on their first contribution. So, by if-ing you are asking them to say *how what they've said with their first contribution bears upon the question*. It *leads* but in a good way: for *inference-making* (see Idea 14).

If the fact

This is when you take an uncertain empirical question (Idea 8) and suppose it to be true or false in order to continue a discussion.

Teaching tip

Don't confuse 'if-ing' with 'what-if-ing'. 'If-ing' is when you take what the pupil has said and put it into a conditional form. 'What-if-ing' (see Idea 58) is when *you* make a suggestion. The former is a contentless questioning strategy, the latter content-full (see Idea 55).

Taking it further

Read the article: 'If it, anchor it, open it up: a closed, guided questioning technique' by Peter Worley. This is the fullest explanation I've so far given of this technique. It is online and open access: www.academia.edu/19271298/If_it_anchor_it_open_it_up_a_closed_guided_questioning_technique.

Key idea: Either-or-the-if

'Let's think about it both ways!'

This is an extension to 'if-ing' (Idea 43) and a very effective way of testing what the pupils say against the overall question being considered, by treating what they say as a variable.

Teaching tip

Look out for the different combinations of response, for example 'yes' to the first 'if', and 'no' to the second. How does that impact on how they answer the overall question? Or vice versa? Or 'yes' to both or 'no' to both?

Taking it further

Read up on thought experiments to see how conceptual variables work: *Wittgenstein's Beetle and Other Classic Thought Experiments* by Martin Cohen (2004) and *What If...* by Peg Tittle (2004) would both be a good starting point. Most of my books show how to bring thought experiments like these into the classroom.

The basic idea here is to take any variable then put (or leave) it in, then take it out and see what its presence or absence does to how the children think. By way of example, say the question is, 'Should the Greeks have gone to war against the Trojans?' (in the *Odyssey*) and someone asks, 'Did Helen go willingly or was she forced to go?' Maybe the story you read wasn't specific about this or maybe you simply don't know! Try 'either-or-the-if'.

To do this, start by saying, 'Well, let's think about it both ways!' Then say, 'So, if she *did* go willingly, for instance if she was in love with Paris, then [anchor] should the Greeks have gone to war against the Trojans?' Wait for a response, then follow with, 'And if she *didn't* go willingly, for instance if she was abducted while sleeping, [anchor] should the Greeks have gone to war against the Trojans?' Where appropriate, remember to follow up 'either-or-the-if' with 'anchoring and opening up' to find out what their responses do to how they think about the overall question. (See 'if-ing', Idea 43.)

'Either-or-the-if' is particularly useful when someone raises a controversial idea. For example, if someone says, 'But Santa/God isn't real!' you can use 'either-or-the-if'. First, ask: 'If Santa/God is real then...[anchor to question]' and then 'If Santa/God is not real then...[anchor to question]'.

Questioning values: 'Do you agree?'

'Questioning values is not just about questioning the values of others but also your own.'

It has become fashionable to refrain from using more traditional stories, especially those with clear, outdated moral lessons. Instead, teachers often opt for the more complex and ambiguous stories, such as those written after and in the spirit of *Where the Wild Things Are* (Sendak, 2000), or updated versions of traditional stories, which often replace one set of old-fashioned values with another set of more up-to-date ones.

Rather than steering children away from the traditional moralistic stories, instead try inviting them to critically engage with these tales. To do so, simply ask them, 'Do you agree?'

Here are a few ways to do this:

- Read the book and ask them if they agree with it, or whether there is anything in the book they agree or disagree with.
- Ask them if they agree or disagree with a particular claim in a book. Sometimes this might come from a character or it might be spelled out in the text (see Aesop's *Fables*).
- Stop the discussion at a *crisis point*, such as when a decision has to be made or just after one has been made, and ask questions such as, 'What do you think X should do? And why?', 'If you were in X's position, what would you do?', or 'Do you agree with what X did?', or 'Was what X did the right thing to do?' This engages the children with the issue when it is still an unknown outcome and so is more likely to engender genuine enquiry, with fewer reflections of 'received beliefs'.

Teaching tip

When getting your pupils to question values, remain in an open questioning mindset (Idea 18). In other words, don't just expect them to arrive at the 'right set of values' that you approve of!

Taking it further

Before asking pupils to critically engage (Idea 47) and make judgements (Idea 24) you may have to address interpretation first. See Ideas 6 and 70.

Key idea: Questioning for arguments

'This [formal argumentation] is something *every* teacher should know about, so why is it not part of teacher training?' (Deputy headteacher)

'Have you answered the question?' is an instruction we all remember from our exam days. This discipline can be encouraged from the very start (nursery) with simple questioning from the teacher. Have the pupils say *what they think* and *why they think it*, making sure they also say *how* what they think bears on the question being considered. In other words, have them construct *arguments*.

First, a little jargon. A **formal argument** is a series of related statements that go to support a claim. The claim that is being made (*what* the arguer thinks) is known as the **conclusion**, and those statements that are offered in support of the conclusion (*the reasons why* the arguer thinks what she thinks) are known as the **premises**.

Example argument:

If you had Christmas every day you'd get bored of it. (Premise)

So, it would be bad to have Christmas every day. (Conclusion)

The word 'so' here indicates that the arguer thinks that the conclusion follows from the premise. That the conclusion is properly (relevantly) connected to the premise(s) is a key feature of an argument.

People (not just children) often say what they think without saying why (e.g. 'CO_2 is the same as air') – that is, they are speaking in **assertions** (unsupported claims). We should get into the habit of questioning to encourage pupils to say not just *what they think* but *why they think it*. If they do both of these, then the children will be both thinking and expressing themselves in argument form, with premises and conclusions.

We can begin this habit early by always opening up assertions, such as the one above about CO_2. So:

- have the Question X ready (Idea 17)
- anchor it (Idea 37), e.g. 'So, is CO_2 the same as air?'
- open it up (Idea 41), e.g. 'Could you say why?'
- if it (Idea 41), anchor it and open it up when necessary, e.g. 'So, if CO_2 is in air, is CO_2 the same as air?'...'Can you say in what way they are different then?'

Writing arguments up

My colleague, Andy West, has a way to encourage critical engagement by writing up arguments that are made so that the children can see the premises that have been invoked to support a conclusion. Take, for example, the following invalid argument (i.e. where the conclusion *does not* follow from the premises):

We breathe in CO_2.

We breathe in air.

So, CO_2 is the same as air.

Then number the premises and conclusion thus:

(1)   We breathe in CO_2.

(2)   We breathe in air.

(1) + (2) = So, CO_2 is the same as air.

The (1) + (2) = helps to show that the statements are linked and that the premises are invoked to support the conclusion. The questions to ask for critical engagement are:

- 'Do you agree with this?'
- Then *pinpoint* with, 'Which bit do you agree/disagree with?'
- Finally, open it up with 'And why?'

Taking it further

Fallacies are arguments that have a superficial look of being good arguments (where the conclusion does follow from the premises), but are actually bad arguments (where it doesn't!). To read more about fallacies, see Weston's *A Rulebook for Arguments* (2018) or Baggini's *The Duck that Won the Lottery* (2008).

Bonus idea ★

Truth and logic: it is really important to understand that an argument can be a good argument without it being true: 'If all astronauts are kangaroos, and all kangaroos are longer than the Nile, then it follows that all astronauts are longer than the Nile.' This is nonsense, of course, but the conclusion *would* follow *if* the premises were true. Here it is in symbols (where the good logic is easier to see): 'If all As are Ks, and if all Ks are L, then all As are L.' 'If-ing' an argument is a good way to test whether it's a logically good (valid) argument. If it is, next ask, 'So, is it true?' In the above case the answer is 'No'.

Questioning for critical thinking

'But if the counter-example is right, then F [fellow pupil] must be wrong.' (Ten-year-old boy)

Critical thinking is not merely the sharing of different opinions, nor is it merely disagreeing with what has been said. It is disagreeing (or agreeing) in the *right* way: about *how* what has been said has been said. It is *evaluative* and *eliminative* and so requires *making judgements* (Idea 24).

Consider the following responses to the question: 'Should people help each other?'

A: I think people should help each other.

B: I disagree, I don't think people should help each other.

At this stage, this is not yet an example of critical thinking, only the sharing of two different opinions, even though B has expressed him/herself as a disagreement. You might think that what's missing is the presence of a *reason*. And, for sure, these responses need to be opened up (see Ideas 24 and 41): 'Could you say *why* you think people should help each other?'

So, once opened up, we might get:

A: I think people should help each other because it's nice to help each other.

B: I disagree. I don't think people should help each other because they can do what they want.

Although there are two arguments now (Idea 24), if this is critical thinking then it is so only in a weak sense. This is because the disagreement from B in no way refers to *what might be wrong* about what A said; it only signifies that

B thinks something different. Here, you should think about *pinpointing* a response with your opening up: 'Could you say what it was A said that you disagree with?'

Then B's response might be:

B: Just because it's nice to help each other doesn't mean that we should always help each other.

Now, this *is* critical thinking because B has taken a critical stance not only to what A has said but to the way in which it has been said, or the *structure* of what they have said. In this case, B has *challenged an inference* (see also Idea 24): they have suggested that it doesn't follow that because it's nice to help each other we should *always* help each other.

However, B has still not provided a reason for his or her point. So, further opening up will help here:

Teacher: Thank you! Could you say why you think that 'just because it's nice to help people it doesn't mean that we should always help each other'? (*Opening up*)

B: Because sometimes you have to be *not nice* to help someone, like in 'cruel to be kind'.

And perhaps even more opening up is needed here, opening up for exemplification (see Idea 41): 'Can you give an example?'

B: Once, my mum shouted at me and made me cry to save me from being run over by a car.

Taking it further

To continue critical engagement in this example, the teacher could *connect*, asking A to respond to what B has said ('right-to-reply' in Idea 19). So, A could say, 'Just because you have to be cruel to be kind sometimes doesn't mean that it's not nice to help others', or the teacher could put it to the class. This might be in general terms: 'Does anyone have anything to say about A and B's discussion?' (see Idea 83) or the teacher might *pinpoint* it: 'Does B's example mean that this is wrong (pointing to A's original statement on the board): "I think people should help each other because it's nice to help each other."?'

Bonus idea

This idea has been adapted from my paper: 'Dissonance: disagreement and critical thinking in P4/wC', International Council of Philosophical Inquiry with Children, 2018, available at www.academia. edu/37155619/ Dissonance_ Disagreement_and_ Critical_Thinking_in_ P4_wC_1 (open access).

Descriptive teaching

'How do you teach a bird to fly?'

Instead of telling children what they should be doing but are not doing, teach them by showing them what they already do.

Some things that you need to teach can be taught *descriptively* (as something the children already do), though they are often taught *prescriptively* (as something that they should do). Examples might be reasoning and inference skills, questioning and formal argumentation (Idea 46). Here are four suggestions for descriptive teaching:

1 Listen out!
Listen for any uses of what it is you wish to teach. Take counter-examples. You may have asked pupils to name things that grow:

Child A: All trees grow.

Child B: Dead trees don't grow. (*Note this counter-example use for when you want to teach it.*)

2 Set them up
Sticking with counter-examples, you could ask, 'What would you say if someone said, "All birds fly"?' I would be surprised if children from around age seven didn't seek a counter-example, e.g. 'penguins'.

3 Build a repertoire
As you gather examples and introduce them to the children, provide a 'thinking wall' from where pupils can select thinking tools or questions (Idea 99).

4 Question
Make a habit of drawing their attention to the repertoire you've gathered. For instance, if someone makes a general claim (see Idea 51), you could say, 'Ah! Someone has made a general claim. Are there any tools on our thinking wall that we could use for general claims?'

Growth mindset

'The whole idea of growth mindset is to say "yes they can".' (Carol Dweck, *Times Educational Supplement,* 26 June 2016)

Growth mindset, developed by Carol Dweck, is a way of thinking, commenting and questioning that draws attention to changeable and controllable aspects of oneself and one's approach to learning. This stimulates agency and self-determination in the pupil to bring about personal development and improvement.

This is sometimes misunderstood as promoting the view that there is no such thing as talent. Growth mindset does not deny natural talent but, through carefully chosen language, draws attention away from aspects one has no power over and towards those things one does have power over (e.g. effort and strategies). It is comparable (though not identical) to the ancient philosophy of Stoicism, nicely captured in the famous Serenity Prayer:

God grant me the serenity to accept the things I cannot change,
Courage to change the things I can,
And wisdom to know the difference.

(Reinhold Niebuhr)

There are many questions online that can be used to promote a growth mindset. However, many of them misrepresent its true spirit and some of them give an oversimplified message: *that you can do anything if you put the work in!* If implementing growth mindset principles, as with anything, take the time to understand it. As Dweck has said, growth mindset is not a simple theory.

There are many ways to promote a growth mindset, but many of the questioning suggestions can be captured in this simple question: 'What action or strategy can you implement to progress or improve?'

Teaching tip

As Dweck herself says, promoting growth mindset is not just putting up a poster, it is embodying the principles in one's everyday classroom practice. A good place to start is to watch out for any evidence of your own 'fixed mindset'!

Taking it further

See Idea 100 about metacognitive questioning, and also research on metacognitive strategies: https://educationendow mentfoundation.org.uk/tools/guidance-reports/metacognition-and-self-regulated-learning.

Socrates and questioning

'Observe, Meno, how I teach using only questions.' (Socrates)

There is a myth in education that the root of the word 'education' (*educare*) actually means to 'draw out from' and not 'stuff in'. This is sometimes cited to show that education has been corrupted over the years.

Teaching tip

Good questions to ask yourself when teaching or when children ask a question:

- Can I get them to teach themselves or answer their own question by questioning them rather than telling them?
- Can I bring them to new knowledge from old knowledge by questioning?

Taking it further

Try to teach a particular thing with only questions and see how far you can get. Note the points at which 'questions only' fails (*if* it fails!) and the points at which something other than questioning is needed (e.g. new knowledge).

Although in fact the Latin *educare* means 'to mould or shape', there is a real history to the myth described above. This notion of education as 'drawing out' can be traced to the ancient Greek philosopher Socrates, or more specifically, to the Platonic dialogue *Meno*. Socrates tries to show his interlocutor, Meno, that learning is really recollecting what was known before in previous lives. Though we may not necessarily share Socrates's belief in previous lives, such things as reasoning and inference-making are capacities we develop without having to be explicitly taught them: in a sense, they are *already in us*. In the dialogue, Socrates attempts to prove his point by teaching a slave boy a solution to a geometrical problem he's drawn in the sand, using only questions. The boy eventually solves the problem.

Some key insights afforded by the *Meno* dialogue are as follows:

- The value of teaching through questioning
- Teaching new knowledge by questioning from old knowledge
- Different kinds of ignorance/knowledge: a) thinking one knows but not knowing, b) not knowing but recognising that one does not know, c) knowing without an account, d) knowing with an account
- The importance of 'losing one's way' or what the Greeks called *aporia* (see Idea 22)

Universal claims

'Everything is relative. Except that.' (Teenage boy)

An important questioning tool is how you question for universal claims using adverbs ('never', 'always', etc.) or determiners ('all', 'none', etc.).

Sometimes, universal/general claims are not explicit and therefore remain either implicit and/or ambiguous. For example, if someone says, 'Trees grow' when asked for an example of things that grow, it is not yet clear whether this is a universal claim ('*All* trees grow').
Imagine a pupil says, 'It's a bird, so it flies.' It would be tempting to infer that the claim – in full – was universal [the square bracket indicates what is inferred and not stated explicitly by the child]:

It's a bird,
[All birds fly,]
So [therefore] it flies.

However, although one would be *logically* justified in making this inference (that 'all birds fly' is indeed what is implied by the logic of the statement), one would not be *psychologically* justified, as it may not accurately reflect what the pupil really intended to say (recall the conversation in Chapter 5 of *Alice's Adventures in Wonderland*: 'Is saying what you mean the same as meaning what you say?'). It is possible the pupil meant:

It's a bird,
[Most birds fly,]
So [therefore], it [probably] flies.

Here, rather than saying, 'So, you think that all birds fly', you may ask them to determine more accurately what they mean, by asking, 'When you said, "It's a bird so it flies", do you think that *all*, *some* or *most* birds fly?'

Teaching tip

It is very important when questioning in this way to maintain an open questioning mindset (see Idea 18): don't lead them, but question them to find out what they think or meant to say.

Taking it further

For more on this, read 'Ariadne's Clew: absence and presence in the facilitation of philosophical conversations' by Peter Worley (2016a) in *Journal of Philosophy in Schools*, 3, (2) (open access).

Modal verbs

'I think maybe it's *maybe*.' (Nine-year-old)

As with universal claims, there's a lot you can do with how you question using modal verbs ('must'/'must not', 'could'/ 'could not', 'should'/'should not', 'might'/'maybe'/'probably', 'definitely'/'definitely not', etc.).

Teaching tip

Use a hand signal to help the younger ones with this: a thumb up for 'definitely', a thumb down for 'definitely not' and a thumb sideways for 'maybe'. See also Idea 89.

Taking it further

Modal verbs are good for practising inferential thinking, e.g. 'If Mr Smith has a bicycle helmet does it mean that he *must have* cycled to school today, that he *must not have* cycled to school today, or that he *maybe* cycled today?'

Sometimes children don't specify the modality of their claim, in which case it can be helpful to offer them some structural guidance, by asking them to qualify modality: 'So, do you think that it *must be* the bear's hat, that it *must not be* the bear's hat or that it's *maybe* the bear's hat?'

Look out for the slightly different functionality of *ethical necessity*: 'You *must* give the money back because it's the right thing to do.'

My colleague Steve Hoggins has a great activity to help develop modal verb thinking with Early Years, through simple questions. He takes a whiteboard and draws a simple object such as a bicycle, part by part, asking at each stage what the children think he is drawing but with the addition of asking them for a modal verb analysis: 'Is it *definitely* a mountain? *Definitely not* a mountain? Or *maybe* a mountain?' He does this with a hand signal, as described in the teaching tip. With each additional part or line he draws, it becomes a little less ambiguous.

Answers and reasons

'It's not a real answer if it's not got a reason.' (Ten-year-old girl)

If someone asks you, 'Do you like raspberry jam?' then you will probably be able to answer this quite quickly with a 'Yes' or 'No'. However, if they ask you, 'Why?' it may be harder to answer: 'Because...I do?' Children, especially the very young, may well be able to provide you with an *intuitive response* such as 'Yes', 'No', 'I don't know' but they may struggle to say why. It is, therefore, important to distinguish between answers and reasons.

It is useful to think of the intuitive response part of an answer to a question (e.g. 'Yes', 'No', 'It depends', 'Maybe', 'I don't know') as separate to what follows – usually indicated with a 'because...'. We are not always immediately aware of *why* we think what we think and it may take a little more time to be able to articulate a reason to an answer that we have provided. Here are some strategies to support that process:

- **Open up.**
Many children will open up for themselves without the need for prompting, for example, 'I think you can have freedom in prison because freedom is in your mind', but for those that don't, ask them, 'Can you say why you think that?' or whatever the appropriate opening up strategy might be (see Idea 41).

- **Give them more time.**
Remind them of the question and wait, perhaps sitting down so as to lower any pressure.

- **Come back to them.**
Allow the discussion to continue and ask the pupil to put up their hand when they are ready to respond. It's good sometimes to prompt them by linking what they say to later contributions.

- **Allow more discussion.**
You may decide to 'target' certain children during talk time to see if a different discussion dynamic yields more.

Teaching tip

Using closed questions allows for *intuitive reflex responses* at least, which, for those who struggle with articulation, is a better starting place than nothing at all.

Taking it further

See Idea 17 about the Question X.

Bloom's taxonomy

'I often see this chart but I'm not sure how to use it.'

Any book about questioning will contain Bloom's taxonomy but it won't necessarily show you how it works practically.

The revised taxonomy (Anderson and Krathwohl, 2001) looks like this:

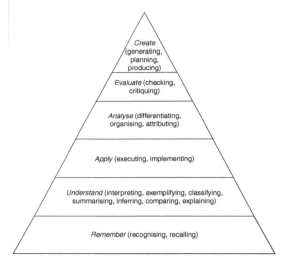

Create (generating, planning, producing)

Evaluate (checking, critiquing)

Analyse (differentiating, organising, attributing)

Apply (executing, implementing)

Understand (interpreting, exemplifying, classifying, summarising, inferring, comparing, explaining)

Remember (recognising, recalling)

This revised version places knowledge *throughout* the taxonomy, and identifies four areas of knowledge:

- *Factual,* e.g. 'What is the solar system?'
- *Conceptual,* e.g. 'What is the difference between numbers and digits?'
- *Procedural,* e.g. 'How do you do long division?'
- *Metacognitive*,* e.g. 'Is my answer close to my (conceptual) estimate? If not, then

* Metacognitive knowledge can itself be broken down into further types (see Idea 100).

there is either something wrong with my (conceptual) understanding or my working out (procedural understanding).'

To illustrate how the taxonomy can be applied to questioning, here is a list of structured questions, based around teaching punctuation:

Lower-order questions

Remember: 'So, what is a full stop?'

Understand: 'Which dot in the following sentence-examples is a full stop?'

Apply: 'Can you/anyone put a full stop in the right place in the following passage?'

Higher-order questions

Analyse: 'Can you say why you would put a full stop here but not here?' Or: 'Why do we use full stops?'

Evaluate: 'Do you agree with X when she put the full stop there? Why not?' Or: 'Is the following a good use of full stops?'

Create: 'Can you think of an example of a sentence where the removal or insertion of a comma changes the meaning of the sentence?'

Taking it further

See also Gallagher and Ascher's questioning taxonomy (1963) and The Sternberg Model (1997 and 2008).

Two types of content

'But Miss, what do *you* think?'

In this book, I refer a good deal to 'contentless questioning', such as if-ing, anchoring and opening up, where the questioning is playing a purely structural role from the teaching/facilitation point of view. However, these strategies do contain content: from the question (wherever that has come from) and from the pupil (what is 'if-ed' will usually come from them). So, should a teacher never provide content?

Of course a teacher should provide content! However, here is a useful distinction: idea-content and curriculum-content.

Idea-content is the substantive content that is *owned* by a speaker and that plays a role in moving a discussion along, usually indicated with the starter 'I think...' (or similar). Someone who represents this kind of content is a 'participant' in a discussion. Often participants will be pupils but sometimes the teacher may inhabit a participant role.

Curriculum-content is that content in the curriculum that the teacher is usually there to deliver. The teacher does not *own* this content; in fact, it may well be at odds with what the teacher thinks. Clearly, it is expected that the teacher will be representing this content in the classroom and, as a pedagogue, will be concerned with how they do this.

So, when I recommend the use of *contentless questions* and *absence* (see also Idea 34) within classroom discussions, it is important to understand that I am not recommending that one represent no content, but:

- to keep the distinction between idea and curriculum content clear
- to be mindful of and monitor one's role as a participant.

Questioning for dissonance

'A controversy often comes from the co-presence of conflict and plausibility.' (Steven Campbell-Harris)

When you want children to see controversies (see Idea 26) or to critically engage with an issue, here is a procedure for doing so that begins in *diversity* (Idea 60) moving towards (cognitive) *dissonance,* based on *dialectical* principles.

1. Begin by asking a grammatically closed but conceptually open (Idea 16) thesis question (Idea 3), such as, 'Was Henry VIII a good leader?'
2. Write the question up on the board.
3. Allow a moment of 'thinking time', a few seconds for pupils to respond to the question silently to themselves. This encourages inner dialogue (see Idea 66).
4. Now allow pupils 'talk time': two minutes talking to the person or people next to them about the question. (See Idea 62 for more on this.)
5. Put your arm in the air to signify the end of talk time.
6. Ask the question again to elicit intuitive responses (see Idea 53).
7. Take responses. At some point, using response detectors (Idea 83), seek a 'Yes' response, a 'No' response and an 'Other' response (this could be 'Yes *and* no', it could be '*neither* yes *nor* no' or it could be a *question* and so on). See Idea 65 for what to do in the case of unanimity.
8. Return to talk time. Now pupils have had an opportunity to hear different positions and – crucially – positions that may conflict but which may also be plausible, they will have more to talk about in talk time and a genuine problem to try to resolve.

Teaching tip

To encourage ownership (see Idea 32) and responsibility (see Idea 23), say that pupils must decide for themselves what they think are the right and the wrong answers based on good reasoning, either their own or that of their classmates.

Taking it further

For more ideas around dissonance and controversy, look at the article 'How to teach controversy in the classroom' by Steven Campbell-Harris (2017): http://www.innovatemyschool.com/ideas/too-close-to-home-how-to-handle-controversy-in-the-classroom.

Key idea: Questioning for the 4 Rs

'It's not enough that we *think* about something; we need to *re-think*.'
(Charles Desforge at an INSET presentation)

Originally conceived to help encapsulate philosophical practice, 'the 4 Rs' has a more general application to teaching, learning and especially *questioning*, which affords it a place in this book.

Teaching tip

It is easy to think of these as *stages* of questioning, but I would recommend thinking of them as *components* or *aspects*. Practically, this means that they may not occur one after the other.

The 4 Rs are:

Respond

When you ask a question, allow for responses with no particular agenda. First, allow a short, quiet 'thinking time' for personal responses. Then allow for responses to each other: firstly with a talking partner (Idea 62), then with the whole class.

Reflect

Very often reflection will begin while responding. Reflection includes asking questions such as:

- What does this question mean?
- What is the question asking?
- What is X? What is meant by X? What do others mean by X? (See Idea 10.)
- Is this the right question?
- Are there more questions to ask in order to answer this one? (See Idea 4.)

Reason

This will usually follow the following structures:

- I think...because...
- If...then...
- Just because...does not mean...
- I disagree/agree with F because..., and so on.

For this part use task and thesis questions (Ideas 2 and 3), making use of strategies such as the Question X (Idea 17) and the related dialectical strategies: if-ing, anchoring and opening up (Idea 43).

Re-evaluate

This is a central value for a 'questioning classroom' – not just *thinking* but *re-thinking* in light of new ideas and information (see 'sensitivity' in Idea 23). To encourage this, ask:

- What do you think now?
- Has anyone changed their mind?
- How do you respond to what F said?
- How would you answer the question now?

Taking it further

Create a template for writing based on this structure using the question suggestions in this idea. See also Idea 66 ('Inner talk').

Bonus idea

Read Descartes' *First Meditation* (a dialogue-in-one-voice) or Plato's *Euthyphro* dialogue (both short!) to see the 4 Rs in action.

Devil's advocate: what-if-ing

'Sympathy for the devil' (The Rolling Stones)

I advise against using Devil's advocate moves elsewhere in this book (see Idea 65), but that does not mean there is no place for this central dialectical move where you entertain a possible objection to an idea or claim.

Teaching tip

Watch out for 'but' when 'what-if-ing': you can 'what-if' without 'but-what-if-ing'! (See Idea 80.)

Taking it further

Philosothon is a movement started in Australia by Matthew Wills, which combines debating competitions with philosophical enquiry. Go here to find out more: https://philosothon.net/.

Bonus idea ★

In the Middle Ages philosophers and theologians held competitive dialectical exchanges called 'disputations', in which two sides would battle it out over an idea (a question or statement) using all the rhetorical devices known to them. Find out more about the *art of rhetoric*, medieval *disputations* and *formal debates*; why not run your own in the classroom? (See also Idea 33.)

Devil's advocate is one of the common 'teacher tics' in class discussion, so I would certainly recommend losing this move *as a tic*. If you use it, do so carefully and deliberately. If you simply fall back on it, you risk doing the intellectual work for the pupils (Idea 65).

Rather, model it and teach it transparently! If using Devil's advocate moves yourself, then tell pupils what you are doing and that you are about to do it. Add it to your 'thinking/strategy wall' (see Idea 99) as a tool *they* can use. Then, where appropriate, task them to use it.

We could call Devil's advocate 'what-if-ing', as it is often signalled with the phrase, 'But what if...?' However, don't confuse this with 'if-ing' (Idea 43). The main difference is to do with content. 'If-ing' is contentless from the teacher point of view (you are 'if-ing' what the pupils have said to encourage inference-making), but 'what-if-ing' (Devil's advocate) brings in idea-content, as the questioner introduces a new idea, scenario or perspective that was not present in the discussion before.

Web of understanding

'Wow!' (Eight-year-old Rokas in response to ten-year-old Noah talking about 'Anti-things')*

Sometimes children say amazing things that leave the others dazed and confused. What do you do if someone says something profound, complex and difficult to follow?

Here is a questioning procedure called the web of understanding, which helps to deepen understanding of a complex idea within the class while minimising the need for you to step in.

- When someone (F) says something complex, begin by asking if there is anyone in the class who thinks they understand what F said. Ask them to say what they think F said *in their own words*.
- Ask F if that is what he or she was trying to say.
- Then ask if there's *anyone else* who thinks they understand. Have them say it in *their* own words.
- Again, ask F to qualify, clarify or correct as necessary.

Be ready to correct or clarify on behalf of F if – and only if – absolutely necessary. Remember that the aim is to step back as much as possible here. If you do need to interpret on behalf of anyone, say, 'Correct me if I'm wrong, but are you saying...?'

Taking it further

A variation of this can be used to have children explain to each other difficult ideas that have been taught to them. Pair up those who understand (As) with those who don't or who are 'on the way' (Bs) and have the As explain to the Bs. When Bs understand, they explain to others. Check that they really do, though!

Bonus idea ★

Check out Singapore Maths approaches: https://en.wikipedia.org/wiki/Singapore_math and Teaching for Mastery: https://www.tes.com/teaching-resources/blog/teaching-mastery-what-mastery for greater understanding of the concepts being taught and used.

* See TEDx Talk 'Plato Not Playdoh' online.

Tasking for diversity

'I have four things to say.' (Ten-year-old Sam)

Sometimes you will be looking for one, specific answer to a question (e.g. 'What is the planetary body that orbits the Earth?'); other times, to generate discussion or controversy, what you need is diversity: a number of different answers.

Sometimes, shifting into an open questioning mindset will be sufficient to elicit a more exploratory mode from the children. However, it can sometimes be helpful to *signal* such a move.

One way to do this is to set children the explicit task of seeking further answers. For example, imagine you use the following to instigate an exploratory discussion on the nature of numbers: **Task question:** How many numbers are there here?

2   2

2   2

(Taken from *The Philosophy Shop* published by Crown House Publishing; Worley, 2012)

One possible problem with this approach is that they all say 'four'. This lack of diversity is going to hinder any further discussion. So, you could 'task' them to seek diversity: 'How many *different* answers to this question can you find?' With this technique, it can sometimes be better to defer opening up (see Idea 41) until after tasking for diversity – that is, if they don't open up for themselves!

Another problem is not that there is no diversity, just that you are not hearing or accessing it. So, if the first few responses to a question such as the above question are similar or the same, simply ask for responses that are 'different from what we have heard before'. (See Ideas 83 and 85; also Idea 65.)

Assumptions: welcome and unwelcome

'Assumptions can be dangerous, but we can't do without them.'

Consider the question: 'Why is it okay to eat animals?' It is making the assumption that it is okay to eat animals. Many would consider that an unwelcome assumption – it may cause offence or a sense of exclusion.

Unwelcome assumptions are generally best avoided. This is especially the case if the teacher thinks it is an assumption that should be accepted, blocking any attempts to challenge it – in which case, the teacher would be inhabiting a closed questioning mindset (Idea 18).

Assumptions aren't always bad. Sometimes they are necessary and sometimes, like dichotomous questions (Idea 9), they can be very effective discussion starters. This depends on the right mindset and aim when using them.

First of all, be aware of any assumptions in your questioning, and if you leave them in, *leave them for a reason*. The question, 'Why should you always be polite?' contains the assumption that we should always be polite. This assumption could in fact be a welcome or an unwelcome assumption. If a child says, 'You shouldn't always be polite' and the teacher says, 'Of course, you should! Now, is there anybody who could explain why?', then this is an unwelcome assumption: one the teacher did not want challenged. However, if the teacher were to say, 'Interesting! Can you give me an example of when you shouldn't be polite?', it might be a welcome assumption, resulting in an assumption being identified by a pupil.

Teaching tip

You can also introduce assumptions with phrases like, 'So, let's imagine...' or, 'Let's suppose...', or by using 'if-ing' strategies (see Idea 43).

Taking it further

Read up on assumptions in a critical thinking book such as *Thinking from A to Z* by Nigel Warburton (2007). And why not teach the class what assumptions are and how to spot them?

Talking partners and groups

'It wasn't me! *He* was talking to *me*.' (Unofficial talking partners)

You will almost certainly have heard of the 'think-pair-share' strategy. This is where the children are expected, in answer to a question, to a) think alone, b) talk to the person next to them, then c) share their answer with the class. This is a good basic strategy, but it's worth having variations of this approach ready to go. Here are five suggestions:

Teaching tip

Quick change! If (and *only* if) they are working in strict pairs, a simple way of having them change their talking partner is to turn *only one person* to a new partner. Everyone should then have a different talking partner.

Taking it further

The book *59 Kagan Structures* (Kagan et al., 2015), from which ideas 1, 2 and 3 were drawn, is well worth a read.

1 **As and Bs:** Assign each member of a talking pair an A or a B. As talk first and Bs second, and while one is talking the other should be listening.

2 **Listening As and Bs:** To ensure good listening from the pair have them share not their own idea but that of their partner (allow their partner to correct or qualify if necessary). And remember transparency (Idea 32): forewarn them!

3 **Time limits:** Give time limits for talking tasks (e.g. 30 seconds for the As to talk and 30 seconds for the Bs). Use any 'egg-timer' app or software to count down.

4 **Think, pair, square, share:** For this, ask children to a) think alone, b) talk to a partner, c) move to groups of three or four (or three *then* four if you want an extra step), before d) sharing with the class. (See also Idea 97 for the question quadrant.)

5 **Listening triads** (Zwozdiak-Myers, 2012): Instead of pairs have trios A, B and C. This is where two of them (e.g. As and Bs) talk while the other, C, listens critically. You could ask C, 'Which one, A or B, did you agree with most?' or 'Which one, A or B, do you think answered the question/task more effectively?' (See also Idea 92 on Socratic circles.)

Hokey Kokey/Kokey Hokey

'In, out, in, out, shake it all about!'

The Hokey Kokey strategy, named after the children's song and based on a Socratic approach, helps move between the *concrete* and the *abstract* to enable you to use one to test the other.

1 Ask a concrete question ('in').
2 Move to its abstract formulation ('out'), such as 'What is X?' (noun form).
3 Return to the concrete to test the abstractions against the concrete ('in' again).

So, in Early Years, it might work like this (with the story *Frog is a Hero* by Max Velthuijs (1997) around the concept-word 'hero'):
1 Is Frog a hero?/Who is the hero in this story?
2 What is a hero?
3 If a hero is…[insert contributions from 1] then is Frog a hero?/Who is the hero?

This can also be reversed to be Kokey Hokey (Thanks, Steven Campbell-Harris!):
1 This time, start with an *abstract* question ('out').
2 Move to a *concrete* formulation ('in').
3 *Connect* abstract formulations to the concrete for testing ('out').
4 Return to the abstract for *re-evaluation* ('shake it all about!').

So, at KS2, Kokey Hokey might work like this (with the curriculum topic Henry VIII around the concept-word 'leadership'):
1 What is a good leader?
2 Was Henry VIII a good leader?
3 If a good leader is…, then was Henry VIII a good leader?
4 So, what is a good leader?

Teaching tip

The Hokey Kokey method makes abstract, exploratory discussions (such as philosophy discussions) useful in other subjects by explicitly linking the abstract considerations to the concrete curriculum-specific question.

Taking it further

See Tim Sprod's 'Foci triangle' (2016) for a three-way understanding of abstract and concrete relationship: https://www.philosophy-foundation.org/blog/in-out-in-out-shake-it-all-about.

Visual thinking strategies (VTS)

'Usually you think with your brain, but sometimes you think with your hands, your ears and your eyes.'

This is a method with questioning at its heart, developed by Philip Yenawine and colleagues (2013) to facilitate a group's ability to appreciate and analyse art. I include it here because it has wide application and transferability, particularly — but not only — for unpacking images of all kinds. VTS also shares the core values of an open questioning mindset (Idea 18).

Teaching tip

A pointing stick may be helpful for pointing to the relevant part of the image when referred to by the children.

Taking it further

Read the book: *Visual Thinking Strategies* by Philip Yenawine (2013) or visit the website: https://vtshome.org/.

As Yenawine says, a VTS teacher helps pupils to:
- look carefully at works of art
- talk about what they observe
- back up their ideas with evidence
- listen to and consider the views of others
- discuss and entertain a variety of interpretations.

Here is a summary of the VTS process:
1 Show the class the image and ask them to look at it quietly for a short while.
2 Ask questions of the group about the image. Good questions would be:
  - What's going on in this picture?
  - What do you see that makes you say that?
  - What more can you find?
3 The teacher then facilitates a discussion by responding to pupils' comments while maintaining a neutral stance. This involves the following:
  - Pointing to parts of the image to clarify which part the children are referring to.
  - Paraphrasing, accurately, each comment.
  - Linking answers and observations that both agree and disagree with each other.
4 To end the lesson:
  - Avoid 'telling them the answer'.
  - Thank them and share something you, as a teacher, 'learned from listening'.

The imaginary disagreer

'Perfect harmony is the enemy of a good conversation.' (Michel de Montaigne)

If children all agree, it is difficult to engender a sustained and fruitful discussion. So, what do you do if there is no disagreement?

If there is 'perfect harmony', you will probably be tempted to resort to 'Devil's advocate' moves, usually beginning, 'But what if...?' (Idea 58). The problem with this is that *you* are then doing the thinking for them. Instead, try to question to activate *them* to do the thinking. If they are very young, it may be because they are not aware of any alternatives, in which case try dichotomous questioning (Idea 9). Or you could try 'Response detector' (Idea 83) to identify children who might hold a different opinion. But if there's *no one* in the room who thinks differently, then try the imaginary disagreer. To employ the imaginary disagreer, invite children to actively *seek out for themselves* an alternative position. Ask:

1 'What do you think someone would say if they disagreed with you?'
2 'What reasons do you think they would give?'
3 'Do you now agree with them?'

There are a number of different ways to bring in the imaginary disagreer:

- If the question is dichotomous ('X or not-X?' or 'X or Y?'): 'What do you think someone would say if they thought not-X/Y?'
- (Role play) 'Character P in the story thinks not-X (or Y), so if you were Character P, why would you think not-X or Y?'
- (Debate-style) 'Can this half of the class think of reasons why X, and this half why not-X or Y?'

Teaching tip

Remember, you will usually only need to find *one person* in the room who has a different view to generate a controversy.

Taking it further

For children who agree with each other, use paired talk: 'What might someone say if they disagreed/think not X/ think Y?'

For the very young, you could use teddy bears: 'Teddy disagrees, he thinks not-X. Can you listen to Teddy and tell me why he thinks not-X?' (Thanks, Steve Hoggins!)

Inner talk

'I think I'm going to disagree with myself!' (Heard many times in good-quality primary school discussions)

The philosopher Socrates — a kind of patron saint of questioning — made an analogy between thinking and talking, suggesting that thinking is a kind of 'silent dialogue'. So, one of the most important questioning approaches is not to do with questioning others but questioning oneself. If we see thinking as a kind of dialogue, good classroom discussions become a model of how to think well.

Various techniques described in this book, notably 'The imaginary disagreer' (Idea 65), encourage forms of inner dialogue. Here are some more ways you can help pupils develop this crucial, metacognitive skill.

What would X say?

Ask what another pupil might say in answer to them or a problem.

Imaginary disagreer

Even the very youngest of children can do this (see Steve Hoggins' use of teddy bears, Idea 65). We have seen children unable to provide a disagreement with their peers but able to disagree with themselves through a teddy bear, suggesting that inner dialogue may come before critical engagement with others.

I think...now I think

Ask pupils to note down at the outset of a discussion an 'I think...' response and then ask them to note down 'Now I think...' at the end. This helps them to be more conscious of their cognitive shifts.

Write dialogues

Finally, the most sophisticated version is to have them write out a short dialogue, as Plato did, between two characters.

Carve it up!

'There's two concepts of free: free to move and free to think.'
(Tyrese, ten-year-old boy)

Being able to draw a distinction is one of the most important critical thinking skills. Put simply, drawing a distinction is when you say what is different between two ideas or what you thought was one idea.

Concept-splitting

The first kind of distinction-drawing is when you take one concept (abstract noun), usually represented by a concept-word, e.g. 'love', and split it into more than one idea, e.g. 'friendship love', 'love of doing things', 'love of humankind'. A good question to ask to encourage this kind of conceptual splitting is: **'Is there more than one kind of X?'** (where 'X' could be 'love' or 'freedom' or 'lying', and so on).

Concept-distinguishing

This is subtly different from concept-splitting. Here, you more clearly separate out different ideas that are often conflated, e.g. 'lying' is not the same as saying what is not true. At first glance they may seem to be the same but you can say what is not true without lying if you tell a fictional story, for example. See also Idea 71 on counter-examples. A good question to ask to encourage concept-distinguishing is: **'Are X and Y the same?'** Try it with the following examples:

- Mind, brain?
- Number, digit?
- World, Earth?
- Water, ice?

Teaching tip

In discussion, there are usually clues that a distinction needs to be drawn. Listen out for expressions such as, 'I think yes *and* no', 'I think *both*', 'I'm in the middle on this', 'Fifty-fifty'. What is often meant by these kinds of expression is *'in a way* X' and *'in a way* not X'. Unpacking them usually reveals a distinction. When you hear these phrases, try asking a distinction-drawing question.

Taking it further

Teach children how to draw distinctions and provide them with a definition on your thinking/strategy wall (see Idea 99).

Answering questions

'All questions have answers even if the answer is "I don't know".'
(Florence, a ten-year-old girl)

There's a useful distinction between *answering* and *responding* to a question that might help Florence (above) make more sense of her interesting observation (thanks, Pieter Mostert!).

Consider the following responses to this question:

How many numbers are there here?

2	2
2	2

(Taken from The Philosophy Shop published by Crown House Publishing; Worley, 2012)

Responses will probably include:

- 'Four!' (Answer with no reason)
- 'What do you mean by number?' (Query about the question)
- 'Well, there are four, but then again, they are the same number, so maybe just one.' (Thinking-out-loud with re-evaluation – see Idea 57)
- 'Two, because even though there are four *digits* on the board they represent the same *number,* and the number is "two".' (Answer with a reason)
- 'Ooh! That's got me thinking!' (Exclamation of engagement and possible recognition of a problem)

All are *responses*, but only some are *answers* in that they attempt to resolve the problem the question has framed. There are two ways that we can understand a question to have been answered beyond merely responding to it: a **candidate answer** and, according to Mostert, **dissolving the problem**.

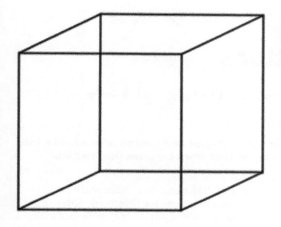

Taking it further

Sometimes children can't answer questions in words, but that doesn't always mean they can't answer a question – they might answer by drawing, acting, pointing, and so on. So, don't forget these options!

Take the following question:

Is this a 2D or 3D shape?

Answers:

- 2D
- 3D
- It is a 2D representation of a 3D shape.

The first two are responses, and answers only in so far as they *say what they think the answer is* (both of which could be understood to be right, though in need of qualification). Only the third response answers the question so that, once understood, as Mostert says, 'it dissolves the problem'. It is, therefore, a *good* answer.

Bad questions

'We were bad. Not bad *good*, but bad *bad*.' (Kermit Ruffins in the TV series *Treme)*

There are bad questions that are just *bad*, and so unworkable, but there are also bad questions that work *because* they're bad.

Teaching tip

Any bad question has value when pupils point out that it's bad and you don't block them or try to cover up. Remain in an open questioning mindset (Idea 18) to get the most out of bad questions.

Taking it further

Ian Gilbert's *The Little Book of Thunks* (2007) is full of good examples of bad questions – in the good sense.

Bonus idea ★

Fermi questions set tricky estimation/ calculation problems with little or no data that are not easy to answer and do not have a settled, determinate answer, e.g. 'How many piano tuners are there in London?' For primary school application, see: https:// www.teachertoolkit. co.uk/2017/04/28/fermi-questions/.

First of all: bad questions. What makes a question a bad question? Here are some suggestions (although there may occasionally be a place for some of them):

- over-complicated questions
- too many questions
- questions that contain contestable yet untouchable assumptions
- (some) leading questions (Idea 14)
- (sometimes) rhetorical questions
- questions asked with a closed questioning mindset (Idea 18)
- questions that are really points being made, not questions
- unclear questions
- (too many) interrogative questions (Idea 13)
- 'weaponised' questions – when a question is used to attack someone.

A **badly asked question** is not always a question bad to ask. Sometimes it is in the 'unpacking' of a badly asked question – establishing *why* it is a bad question – that we may find the good in a bad question.

Vague questions, as long as they are vague in the right way, can be treated in a similar way. Leaving terms deliberately wide open invites the group to fill them in with a 'What do you mean by X?' question (see Idea 41).

Some questions might be considered bad because they contain **assumptions**. However, that all depends on what kind of assumption it is and how we treat the assumptions (Idea 61).

Questioning for interpretation

'What *happened* is one thing; what it *means* is another.'

This method for critical interpretation of texts is adapted from a Jewish approach to textual interpretation known as PaRDeS, where texts have four levels: 1) literal, 2) moral, 3) metaphorical and 4) hidden.

Try this process to question for interpretation:

1 **Read** the text or present the image.
2 For a **literal** interpretation, ask, 'What happened in the text?' / 'What do you see?' (See Taking it further.)
3 To bring them to a **moral** (virtue-oriented) interpretation, ask, 'What, if anything, do you think we are supposed to learn from the story/image?'
4 To **critically engage** them with a **peer's interpretation**, ask, 'Do you agree with [name] that the story is about [insert interpretation in child's words not yours]?' e.g. 'Do you agree with Mary that the story is saying "Follow your dreams!"?'
5 To **critically engage** them with the **suggested moral**, ask, 'Do you agree that [insert identified moral]?' e.g. 'Do you agree that you should "follow your dreams"?'

Sometimes the class will take itself to a **metaphorical** reading of the text, e.g. 'When the character has a dream that tells him to follow his dreams, it's really himself telling him to do that because his dreams come from his own head.' This is to be distinguished from the moral level in that it is not necessarily to do with how we should live or behave but about understanding human nature through metaphor. See also Idea 64 on visual thinking strategies.

Teaching tip

Use the descriptive approach to teaching (Idea 48) to teach the different levels of a text.

Taking it further

At stage 2, to encourage summary of texts, set the following task: 'Can you say what happened in the text in less than x words?' (20 words, ten words, five words, three words or even *in one word!*). Depending on the class's interpretative abilities, this exercise itself can bring them to interpretation (e.g. 'Follow your dreams!' or 'Loss'). See also Ideas 6, 40 and 64.

Counter-examples

'Dead birds *can* fly if you take a roast chicken on an aeroplane.' (11-year-old)

A counter-example is a critical thinking tool and is defined as 'an example that refutes a general claim' (for children: 'that goes against a general claim').

Teaching tip

To help manage counter-examples, use atomic anchoring (Idea 39):

a) 'So, is it an example?' then b) 'Does it go against a general claim? If so, what general claim?'

Taking it further

Read my article 'How to introduce critical thinking into your classroom' available for free on the Innovate My School website: http://www. innovatemyschool.com/ ideas/how-to-introduce-critical-thinking-skills-into-your-classroom.

Ask the class what they would say if someone said, 'All birds fly.' You are likely to hear some counter-examples, e.g. 'Penguins don't fly.' Sometimes children will naturally provide such counter-examples, but at other times, you will need to prompt them to do so:

- **Write the general claim on the board:** e.g. (explicit) 'All numbers are either odd or even'; (implicit) 'To be real you've got to have a heartbeat'; (implied general claim) 'All real things have heartbeats.'
- **If they know what a counter-example is, ask:** 'Can anyone think of a counter-example, an example that goes against this general claim?' [*Point to the claim on the board.*]
- **If they don't know what a counter-example is, ask:** 'Can anyone think of something that is X but is not Y?', e.g. 'Can anyone think of something that is real but that does not have a heartbeat?'

Counter-examples both eliminate poorer answers and help to produce better answers. For example, if Sam makes the claim, 'All trees grow,' someone may object with 'But trees made into furniture don't grow,' to which Sam has to reject or revise his first claim: 'I meant all *living* trees grow.' But remember, not all counter-examples are good ones. Though 'penguins' is a successful counter-example to the claim, 'All birds fly', 'flamingos' is not and 'chickens' inhabits a grey area. (See also Idea 51.)

Question
delivery

Part 4

Key idea: Putting into question

'To be or not to be: that is the question.' (Hamlet)

We don't always have to ask questions to 'ask questions'. You may recall how the 'question' you were supposed to answer during your university exams was very often not in question form at all, but in the form of a quote followed by the instruction, 'Discuss'.

Teaching tip

When eliciting 'questions', listen out for controversial statements. I call this the 'Quote-Discuss' approach, after the exam technique.

Taking it further

Debating (Idea 58) can be a fun and structured way to explore a question through statements and how one responds to statements, either to defend or refute them. A useful resource *Primary Debating Handbook* by Concern Worldwide is available free online at www.concern.net/sites/default/files/media/page/primary_debating_handbook_a5_updated.pdf.

The 'quote' in an exam question raises a controversy that it is your job to illustrate, explore and make a judgement about. The issue, by virtue of being a controversy, is *put into question*. That's why we still call it a question, and rightly so. J. T. Dillon, in his book *Using Discussion in Classrooms* (1994), makes sense of this by drawing a helpful distinction between 'asking questions' and 'putting *into* question' (see Idea 25).

Consider the following two ways of presenting an issue: A) 'Do you think girls are better at some things than boys and vice versa?' B) 'Girls are better than boys at solving problems in teams.' (*The Independent*, 22 November 2017) Example B is more likely to get a visceral response, making the debate come alive. Example A, carefully, doesn't assume anything and that could be what holds any ensuing discussion back from finding what Steve Hoggins terms a 'bite point'.

Shakespeare is a master of 'putting things into question' without peddling an obvious agenda, by *showing* rather than *telling*. *The Merchant of Venice* shows us antisemitism, but it is, arguably, not an antisemitic play. Shakespeare *puts into question* the prevailing Christian values by first giving us the 'Quality of mercy speech' and then having the Christians 'show no mercy' in their triumph over Shylock.

Guided questioning vs. non-guided questioning

'Sometimes a map is better, but sometimes it's good to find your own way.'

An attentive reader may well have noticed elsewhere in this book the importance I put on guided, structured questioning where the questioning demands a very specific answer. However, non-structured questioning is also valuable. So, when should you carefully structure your questioning and when should you not?

A good example is the exercise In Idea 71 around the statement 'All birds fly'. By writing this statement on the board or by saying it, you invite the class to 'put into question' the statement. Having done this, step back; see what happens! Either wait for a response (or raised hand) or allow talk time. The careful, structured questioning you see outlined in Idea 71 is only necessary *when it is necessary*.

Another good example would be opening up (see Idea 41). In many cases, especially with older, more confident and eloquent children, opening up will be unnecessary as they will do it for themselves: 'Is war ever a good thing?' 'No, because...' And, even when this does not happen straight away, very often it will, given time: 'Is war ever a good thing?' 'No.' [*wait-time applied*] Pupil continues, '...because...' (See 'Wait-time' in Idea 41).

Also see 'if-ing for inferencing' in Idea 43, as here you see exactly when structured questioning is required: if the child, when you anchor them, does not follow through the implication of their first idea in relation to the question, 'if' them in order to make a slightly greater demand in terms of how you expect them to relate their second answer to their first.

Teaching tip

Step back! You will find that, by looking for opportunities to step back, there will be many more opportunities than you might at first think. Then, when necessary, step in.

Taking it further

See my papers 'If it, anchor it, open it up: a closed, guided questioning technique' and 'Ariadne's Clew: absence and presence in the facilitation of philosophical conversations' (both available online for free at https://peteworley. academia.edu/).

Sequential questioning

'You can't run before you can walk!' (Proverb)

An important but difficult skill in questioning is asking questions clearly and *in the right order*.

Sometimes you need to answer other questions before you can answer the question you've been asked. A good questioner is sensitive (see Idea 23) to these further questions (see Idea 4) and makes them explicit as and when necessary.

Here, a music teacher is teaching a pupil with careful, sequential questioning, a new piece:

1 What is the note here called?
2 [*Whether correct or incorrect*] Can you show me how you worked it out?
3 [*If not known*] Are there any other notes on this page that you *do* know?
4 [*If 'yes'*] What notes do you know?
5 [*Once established*] Is the note we started with lower or higher than the note you know?
6 How many steps higher?
7 So, if it is three steps higher than the A, what note would it be?
8 Do you know how to work that out? Do you know the scale? Remember: 'scale' means 'ladder', so climb the ladder three steps to see what the note is.
9 So, what is the note here called?
10 That's right! D.

Whys words: asking why

'Can you say why?' 'Why.' (Me to a five-year-old, then the five-year-old to me)

What is the difference between 'Why?' and 'Tell me your reasons!'? You may say that the former is a *question* and the latter a *command*. So, is *why* a question or a disguised command? Or both?

Some people have suggested that 'Why?' is an aggressive – even violent – word and that it should therefore not be used in certain circumstances (such as some kinds of therapy). Just consider how you feel after a six-year-old has asked you, 'Why?' a number of times in succession. It can be exhausting! However, it is simply too important in the classroom to do without. So, it is helpful to consider the different ways that 'Why?' functions. There are four 'whys':

- **The *causal* why:** This is where you ask someone to explain the circumstances that brought something about, e.g. 'Why did the water turn into steam?'
- **The *justification* why:** This is where you ask someone to provide the reasons that support a claim or conclusion, e.g. 'Why (for what reasons) do you think that eating meat should be made illegal?'
- **The *purpose* why:** This is where you ask someone to state the overall aim or goal of something, e.g. 'Why (what for?) did you use that particular strategy?'
- **The *motivation* why:** This is where you ask someone to provide the reasons that made them do or say something (a psychological version of the 'causal/purpose why' that is significant in helping us understand how 'why?' impacts on a class), e.g. 'Why did you get up?'

Teaching tip

Don't remove 'why?' from your vocabulary, but do 'soften it'. Instead of just asking, 'Why?', which can be aggressive, ask, 'Would you mind saying why you think that?' or 'Can you say your reasons for that?' and so on.

Taking it further

Why not explain the differences between 'the four whys' to the class and have them attempt to say which kind of why they are asking or answering?

Know why you're asking a question

'I knew I had a point!' (That moment when we lose our thread!)

I prefer to split this into two: knowing *why* you are asking a question, and knowing why you are *really* asking a question.

Having a clear purpose to your question-asking is the first step to improving your questioning. For example, (drawing on Bloom's taxonomy, Idea 54) are you after *recall*, e.g. 'What is bigger, an atom or a molecule?', or are you after *evaluation*, e.g. 'Do you agree with X when she said...?'

This will help with clarity, concision, accuracy, appropriateness and answerability. However, in addition to this analysis, you also need to ask yourself what your *mindset* is, or what your *real* purpose is. Is it to hear them say what *you're* thinking or looking for (closed questioning mindset, Idea 18), or is it to hear them say what *they* are thinking (open questioning mindset)?

You may well ask what on the surface seems like an evaluation question: 'Do you agree with Mary that everyone should cooperate?' But underlying the question is a hope that they will agree because you think that Mary is right. There are two things to bear in mind here:

- You may well reveal what you expect in ways other than the question you ask, e.g. by tone, facial expression, or body language.
- You may have let your own view limit your understanding of the issue. For example, you may have failed to think of alternatives to Mary's view *because you think it's right*, or you may not be open to problematising Mary's view (Idea 26), such as not properly listening for alternative ideas from others.

Use clean questions or even none at all!

'There's a double meaning in that.' (Benedick, in *Much Ado About Nothing*)

It is very common to make a statement such as, 'So, you think that the Greeks should not have gone to war against the Trojans', when what is really meant is the question: 'So, *do you think* that the Greeks should have gone to war against the Trojans?' The statement asks more work of the listener to figure out what is required, leading to possible misinterpretation and misunderstanding.

The second example above is a 'clean' question because it is more direct and transparent. If you want to ask a question, then *ask a question*. (An important exception would be where you want to put something *into question,* see Idea 25.)

If you think that the children are not sticking to the rules of a game, discussion, etc., you might ask, 'So, children, are we sticking to the rules?' This is *not* clean because the question is really a statement of your intent phrased as a rhetorical question: 'I don't think you are sticking to the rules and I think we need to address this.' A cleaner question would be: 'Some people are not sticking to the rules. What can we do to fix this?'

However, a question might not be appropriate at all: 'Some people are not sticking to the rules. Let's go through them again to make sure they're clear.' Teachers often feel that they must say everything *as a question,* ensuring their teaching is pupil-centred. However, this can result in an over-complex psychological classroom culture where the children spend a lot of time 'mind-reading' to work out what the teacher is really asking them or trying to say (see also Idea 18).

Teaching tip

Be in the habit of speaking clearly, transparently (Idea 32) and directly.

Taking it further

Read this book about asking questions, in a therapy context, in a way that minimises implicit or rhetorical force to avoid misunderstanding: *Clean Language: Revealing Metaphors and Opening Minds* by Judy Rees and Wendy Sullivan (2008). See also cleanlearning. co.uk.

Be precise and thorough

'Say what you mean and mean what you say.'

If you want someone to say what they think about something, don't ask, 'So, what do you *feel* about what X said?' Conversely, if you want someone to report their emotional response, don't ask, 'What do you *think* about that?' Say exactly what you mean.

Teaching tip

If you are not absolutely clear in your own head about how to phrase or formulate a question, then don't ask it yet. Give yourself time to get it right.

Taking it further

You can reverse this principle, as sometimes you may want to make a question deliberately ambiguous (see Idea 2).

Very often we do not ask questions in their complete form. For example, 'Do you like Marmite?' is really: 'Do you like the taste of Marmite?' Sometimes a full question does not need to be asked as the meaning is easily inferred from the context. However, the questioner should be aware of what the full question really is, whether or not it is asked explicitly, so that one can make the question more explicit if necessary, such as when you ask a question to very young children.

Imagine asking, 'What is 2 + 2?' in the following two scenarios:

1 A maths lesson where you are teaching children how to add numbers between 1 and 10
2 A philosophy lesson about language and meaning with adults.

In the first case 'What is 2 + 2?' will function perfectly well, standing in for 'What is the total of the sum 2 + 2?' with no need for further explication. However, in the second case, the question 'What is 2 + 2?' could be understood very differently; it could be construed as, 'What is the function and meaning of the statement 2 + 2?' Or, if you were to ask, 'Do you like Marmite?' in the context of a media studies university class, you might need to be clearer and more explicit about whether, for example, you wanted to know if the students like the *brand* 'Marmite'.

The question razor: eliminate the unnecessary

'?' (The necessary question?)

When we question, we often ask too many questions, or our questions become too complicated and long-winded. In most cases, it would be better to shorten and simplify a question.

Here are some ways of simplifying questions:

- **Anchor:** When you have a good, clear question, simply anchoring to it will work in many situations. For example, instead of something like, 'So, going back to the original question, what does that have to do with the question?', just anchor (Idea 37) back to the question: 'So, is it ever acceptable to harm someone else?' Then, stop talking and listen! (See Idea 21.)
- **Remove idioms:** For example, 'Can you expand/elaborate on that?' can be simplified to 'Can you say more?'
- **Remove complex language:** 'So, how does that relate to the question?' to a Year 3 child is likely to leave them unsure as to how to respond. Instead, just anchor back to the question: 'So, do you think it's okay for the lion to lie?'
- **Look for basic structures:** Ask yourself, 'What is the basic question I want to ask?' and try to understand it as a structure to help eliminate all the padding in a question that we so often reach for, e.g. 'What is X?', 'Is X the same as Y?', 'Is X more important than Y?' and so on. (See Idea 10.)
- **Contentless questioning:** This is where you shave off all your own *idea-content* (see Idea 55) so that you perform only a structural role in your questioning.

Teaching tip

When you question, always ask yourself, 'Can my question be simpler?'

Taking it further

You may want to apply the razor to what you say in general, not just with questions. Ask yourself: 'Do I really need to say this?' or 'Could I say it more succinctly?'

Sit on your 'but'

'Yes, and...' (Improvisational comedy game)

When questioning in follow-up to things pupils say, it is *very* easy to slip a 'but' in, giving the impression what has been said is irrelevant or wrong. Generally speaking, try to remove your 'buts' and say 'and' or 'so' instead. Unlike removing 'Why?' (see Idea 75), nothing is lost.

Teaching tip

Another common tendency is to use the word 'but' as we talk over someone. Try to avoid this!

Taking it further

Find out more about 'Yes, and...'-thinking, a rule of thumb in improvisational comedy that has become an influential idea in business, too. Then, when you are next asked a question that tempts you to begin your response with 'But...' imagine you are playing 'Yes, and...' and re-think your response. If introducing this idea to your colleagues, play the game in a staff meeting!

Compare the following two teacher responses in this anchoring move (see Idea 37):
Child: CO_2 is *in* air.
Teacher: *So*, is CO_2 the same as air?
Or:
Teacher: *Yeah but* is CO_2 the same as air?
The first response says: 'What can you infer regarding the question from what you have said?', whereas the second response suggests, 'Okay, so CO_2 is *in* air but that doesn't mean that it's the same thing as air, right?' The second 'leads' in the wrong way: *rhetorically*; the first leads in the right way: *inferentially*. The second is doing the intellectual work *for them*; the first has the pupils do the intellectual work. (See also Idea 14.)

One very good reason to adopt the 'and' or 'so' principle is that one should resist prejudging relevance. Take this example:
Child: I made cakes at the weekend.
Teacher: Yeah but what's that got to do with the question: is CO_2 the same as air?
Child: Well, ingredients are in a cake but they are not the same thing as a cake. It's the same with CO_2 and air.
In this case, the teacher would have done well not to assume the contribution was irrelevant!

Invisible punctuation

'Why do we need punctuation? It's not there when you speak.'
(Eight-year-old girl)

Many people will be familiar with the well-worn example of seeing how punctuation changes the meaning of a sentence:

'Let's eat Nan!'

'Let's eat, Nan!'

Emphasis *alone* can change the meaning of a question. Look at the different kinds of responses these different emphases can engender:

- *Why* shouldn't he eat his cat? ('Because he loves it.')
- Why *shouldn't* he eat his cat? ('Because it's wrong to eat cats.')
- Why shouldn't *he* eat his cat? ('Because his starving children need it more.')
- Why shouldn't he *eat* his cat? ('Because it would make a better hat.')
- Why shouldn't he eat *his* cat? ('Because his neighbour's cat is tastier.')
- Why shouldn't he eat his *cat*? ('Because his dog is more nutritious.')

To avoid asking leading questions, which can be achieved with tone and emphasis (Idea 14), one would normally avoid putting emphasis on a question. However, when approached as an intentional exercise, this can be a valuable way of finding out what else a question can yield without changing a word. Try the following: take a question – any question – and repeat it with a different emphasis to see what impact that has on how the class respond to it or understand it. With some questions, it will do very little, but with others it can change everything (see the first two responses above).

> **Teaching tip**
>
> Keep an eye on your own emphases when questioning; *emphasis* has the power to make a question or statement into its opposite! Avoid using this technique covertly, but certainly make use of it overtly to get more out of questions.

Speaker
selection

Part 5

Questioning radar: spears or nets

'One of the basics of good teaching.'

When you question a class, to whom should you direct your question? Should your 'questioning radar' be narrow like a spear or wide like a net?

Of course, the answer to the question above will depend on what you are trying to achieve with your questioning, but here are some considerations.

Even when directing your question to one child, keep your radar wide open and address the rest of the class by considering your eye-contact, stance, hand gestures, tone, and so on. An open radar takes the pressure off the pupil being questioned while enlisting the others to be ready to help, as well as keeping them engaged.

A narrow radar targets one child, usually with a closed question (Idea 16), and the questioner often adopts certain kinds of body language such as craning the neck forward, walking towards the child, looking only at one child, and using interrogative questions (Idea 13). These tendencies often accompany a closed questioning mindset (Idea 18). This can alienate the majority of the class as they will feel that, unless they are being questioned directly, they are not part of the discussion.

Response detector

'Penguins have an almost magical way of finding their chicks in amongst millions of other penguins.'

Sometimes taking a response is not enough — you need to find the one or more children who have something to say that has the right dialectical connection to what went before, so you need a way of detecting particular kinds of responses. (See 'Dialectic' in Idea 29.)

On occasions in the past, I have thought to myself, 'This discussion is not really going anywhere or I'm not hearing the insight that would help the discussion progress,' so I've suggested something to move things along. And, on some occasions, a child has said to me afterwards, 'When you said..., I was going to say that!' This made me think that I should have found a way to access that particular idea, rather than saying it myself, prematurely.

So, here it is: **the response detector**. This is a way of identifying a particular kind of response, e.g. a disagreement, a connected idea to a previous speaker or question, a 'No'. For example, imagine that the first few respondents say the same thing, e.g. 'Bigger presents are the best presents', in answer to the question, 'What are the best kind of Christmas present?' You may find yourself tempted to make an alternative suggestion to them, or you could try to *detect* those in the room who may provide the alternative position so that you don't have to: 'Is there anybody who has a different answer to those who have already spoken?'

The **antithetical response detector** is when you look specifically for someone who thinks not just differently but in some kind of opposition. So, if the first three responses were all, 'It is fair,' you might ask, 'Is there anyone who thinks that it's *not* fair?'

Teaching tip

Never say idea-content (Idea 55) in classroom discussions if you can find a way of checking whether someone in the class was going to say the same thing.

Taking it further

See Idea 85 for ways to make your specifications even sharper.

No hands!

'No hands doesn't mean: *no thoughts!'*

You've asked a question but there are no hands up. Though this is more common in secondary schools than primary, always be prepared for this outcome.

Here are some practical suggestions to help if no one wants to answer.

Talk time: Almost always give time to talk to each other about a question before requesting responses. This should also be done if you want pupils to ask questions to you or a speaker. Tell them explicitly that during talk time they should try to come up with at least one question in their pairs or groups.

Listen: During talk time, walk around and listen in to what's being said. Have small chats with groups and pairs, being careful not to dominate or take over. Stick to simple, clean, contentless questions. Make notes of who has said what and use this time to target the less forthcoming children. Now you have some idea of what they are thinking and who you can go to.

Invite: Ensure that the culture of your classroom is one where the children feel they can always contribute and that you are interested in *what they think* (see Idea 18). More specifically, invite those in whose ideas you've already heard during talk time. If it will help to take the pressure off one person, invite them to speak as part of their pair or group.

Connect: Invite those in who have ideas that bear a dialectical relationship to the ideas that have already been voiced, perhaps a challenge, building on what's been said or providing a new perspective.

Hands up if..., hands down if...

'A kind of thinking aerobics with real aerobics!'

Sometimes – and it's great when this happens – the problem is not that pupils *won't* put their hand up but that *everyone* does! This can be overwhelming and it's easy to miss children so that some get several goes in a discussion and others none.

Here's a 'handy'(!) technique to help manage this situation. The default version is to allow *hands up of all those who want to speak* described in Idea 84. Then, with the 'hands down if...' part, stipulate and narrow down. So, 'Hands down if you've spoken already,' or, later, 'Hands down if you've spoken more than once.'

Another common situation is: 'Hands up if you've not spoken but would like to; hands down if you've spoken already.' Though the second clause is implied in the first, it sometimes needs to be made more explicit, hence the repetition. You can also use alternative methods for speaker selection to 'Hands up' (see Idea 88).

Teaching tip

Often remind the class that 'everyone is invited to speak', that you can 'only hear from one person at a time' and that 'their patience is appreciated'. Also, regularly come back to (especially towards the end of the lesson): 'Is there anyone who has not spoken today and would like to?'

Taking it further

This technique can also be used as a form of **response detector** (Idea 83). So, for example, 'Hands up if you'd like to respond to [name of previous speaker]; hands down if you've spoken already.' Or, 'Hands up if you think that you should do X, but you've got a different reason to F?'

Quiet children

'_____' (Many children in classroom discussions!)

'Come on! We haven't heard anything from you today. You must have some thoughts!' Putting children on the spot in this way is not very helpful.

Teaching tip

Be aware! It's very easy to allow the dominant speaker to dominate, especially if they are saying interesting and relevant things. Check yourself from time to time and look around. What are the others doing? Less forthcoming pupils often give you clues, such as a slightly raised arm, sitting forward, or, less obviously, just a look in the eye.

Taking it further

Most quiet children *will* speak, given the right conditions, so think hard about the culture and environment the pupils find themselves in when in your classroom. See also Idea 19.

Here are some ways that you might be able to 'draw them in' and consequently draw more out from them.

- **Invite** them to speak from time to time (see Idea 19).
- **Target** quiet children during talk time. Listen attentively and look for opportunities to use what they say constructively.
- If you have gathered ideas from quiet children during talk time, then **bring those ideas into the discussion** during class discussions.
- **Ellipsis...:** 'Conveniently forget' their idea but make sure you have at least one key word or phrase, e.g. 'Sasha, you were saying something very interesting about "fault and responsibility"...what was it?' Notice also those encouraging words, 'something very interesting...'.
- **Anchor** them to the question (see Idea 37). All you need is a simple 'yes' or 'no', or even a nod or shake of the head, and you have some kind of answer. To get more, open them up (see Idea 41). Even if they offer no more than a shake of the head, *it is at least something*. And if it turns out to be the only answer of its kind (e.g. the only 'No' to the question) you can return to it later.
- Always **thank** speakers for their contributions, use their names often and **listen actively** (see Idea 21).

Visual polls

'We want our thumbs!' (Bill Hicks, comedian)

In your class, there are approximately 30 minds hidden from you. During discussions, finding a method of having everyone in the class represent their position visually and simultaneously is often a good way of getting a 'starting sense' of what's in those minds.

Having everyone indicate their reaction at the same time gives an instant sense of 'the thinking landscape', i.e. whether the particular issue is controversial and to what extent, as well as who holds the main positions ('Yes', 'No', 'Both', and so on).

It's common to ask, 'Who agrees?' and/or 'Who disagrees?', but if you ask just one of these (or if you ask both) you only address those that either agree or disagree. They might *kind of* agree, *neither* agree *nor* disagree, *both* agree *and* disagree or they might have another point to raise altogether.

The **thumb poll** can help with this. Use the thumb (or similar signal) to represent simple positions to statements or claims: a thumb up for 'I agree' or a thumb down for 'I disagree' and a thumb to the side for other positions. 'Other positions' might include 'I don't know', 'I'm not sure', 'Both', 'Neither', 'Something different', 'Maybe'.

Teaching tip

If you are uncomfortable with a thumb up or down when they are representing their views on something a peer has said, then use a different signal to indicate agreement or disagreement. However, if you have established trust in the classroom, the thumb poll shouldn't be a problem.

Taking it further

Type 'hand signal posters for classroom' into your search engine and you will find many online suggestions.

Bonus idea ★

Jason Buckley (www.thephilosophyman.com) has the children take a space in the room to represent their position. Have them stand close to a statement for agreement and further away for disagreement (like a magnet). They should decide how near or far they stand.

Hands up? Speaker selection

'I'm just stretching!' (Thousands of children over the years)

When you ask a question, should you take *hands up* responses? Some schools have banned 'hands up' in classrooms. We put hands up in answer to questions to show that we have a response to the question. However, not everyone who has something to say will put their hand up and not everyone who puts their hand up will necessarily have something (sensible) to say.

I don't recommend banning 'hands up', as this method for question selection performs an important dialectical role: it keeps contributions appropriately connected to each other. However, simply falling into the default habit of taking *only* questions from those with hands up is also unsatisfactory. Any speaker-management method, whether hands up or random selection using lollipop sticks, has its own bias or problems – for example, hands up often results in the same speakers and lollipop sticks can result in unsatisfactory random relationships between answers, especially in discussions.

Here are some common ways to select speakers:

Hands up! Hands down!

This is the most common form of speaker selection and it is valuable (see above). However, listening is poorer when people have their hands up as they will be thinking about what they are going to say or willing the teacher to pick them. For this reason, I prefer to insist that hands are kept down until the current speaker has finished. I have found this improves the listening and creates a calmer atmosphere in the classroom. Many teachers prefer other ways of achieving what 'hands up' achieves: some use 'palms out' or 'thumbs up' to indicate that someone wants to contribute.

Random selection

Many readers will be familiar with the popular lollipop-stick method referred to above, where pupils' names are each written on a lollipop stick and placed in a pencil holder. When a teacher wants everyone to be ready to answer a particular question, he or she simply picks a stick out to determine who is to give the answer. It is, as the title suggests, very random but it certainly has its place in eliciting something from those who are not the usual suspects.

Taking it further

Observe yourself (or have someone else observe you) selecting speakers. Do any patterns emerge? Are there any biases? What are your speaker selection habits? What should you change?

Pupil selection

This is where the children select the next speaker, giving them control and you a break! There are some problems with this: children often select their friends, or they select only children of the same gender. If using the pupil selection method, you will need to keep an eye on these things and, until the class can manage this themselves, you may prefer to carefully control how it's done. For example, you may say, 'When each person finishes, choose someone who has not spoken already and who is [of the opposite gender].' This could be done with or without hands up.

Some more in brief

- **Peer help:** If someone gets stuck while attempting to answer, you could ask, 'Is there anyone who thinks they might be able to help X?'
- **Invitation (individual or group):** Ask pupils whether they would like to say something in response to a question or another speaker. Make sure that it is an invitation.
- **Invitation with anchor-to-prompt:** Sometimes an anchor-to-prompt (see Idea 38) is needed if they simply shrug.
- **Response detector:** This can be useful when you need a specific kind of response (see Idea 83).
- **Gender alternation:** Switch between girls and boys – not necessarily rigidly 'girl, boy, girl, boy', but make sure you get a good overall balance.

Hand signals

'I wanted to say something but it's passed now.' (Many children – with aching arms)

It becomes increasingly difficult to follow the dialectical demands of a conversation with larger numbers of children (see Idea 29). Hand signals, where the meaning of each signal is agreed within the class, are one way you can tackle this.

Teaching tip

Don't introduce all these hand signals at once, but gradually. Perhaps make a chart of hand signals for the wall. You can find examples and posters by searching online for 'hand signal posters for classroom'.

Taking it further

Have pupils learn to *articulate* what kind of response they are giving by providing them with vocabulary: i.e. qualification ('I agree but...'), add to ('I agree and...'), inference challenge ('Just because... doesn't mean that...'), and so on. Thanks, Andrew Day!

Hand signals help the teacher determine, before selecting, what kind of response the class will hear. In addition, the children are encouraged to characterise/categorise what kind of response they will give, which helps to develop a metacognitive attitude towards contributions. As well as thinking about *what kind of contribution* it will be, they also think about *what kind of impact* it might have, and about *what would be the appropriate response* (see Idea 23).

Some children may use the hand signal to fast-track themselves to 'getting a go' sooner and some will use the hand signal to please the teacher. The clue that these are the motivations is in the quality of the response, for example when the hand signal is not an indication of the kind of response they give. Have them explain how what they say is what the hand signal indicates.

Here are some suggested hand signals – you can also make up your own:

- **Question:** make a 'Q' sign.
- **Counter-example** (see Idea 71): make a 'C' sign.
- **Distinction** (see Idea 67): make a 'D' sign.
- **Inference** (see Idea 24): tap forefinger against palm of other hand.
- **Response to a previous speaker:** a lone forefinger when hand is up.
- **Add to:** make a plus sign.
- **I agree:** tap left shoulder with right hand.

Building children's questioning and enquiry skills

Part 6

Philosophy and P4C

'Philosophy is more about understanding questions than just asking them.' (Ten-year-old girl)

Philosophy helps children explore, ask and answer questions in a reflective way.

P4/wC (Philosophy for/with Children), is a catch-all term for a general approach based on Matthew Lipman's and Anne Margaret Sharp's teachings about doing philosophy with children in a community of inquiry (see Idea 31). There are also other approaches, some closely aligned to Lipman's original work and some less so – see, for example, McCall's CoPI (2009), Sapere's P4/wC, Haynes and Murris (2012), Buckley and Bigglestone's 'Philosophy Circles' (2016), Shapiro (2012), Cam (2006), Wartenberg (2014) and Worley (2011b and 2015a).

Here are the main approaches outlined. PhiE and CoPI are both facilitated, generally, by philosophers and P4/wC is facilitated, generally, by class teachers.

Lipman/Sharp P4C (Philosophy for Children)

1 A section of one of Lipman's philosophical novels is read by a group of children.
2 At a certain point in the narrative, the children stop reading to do some exercises to develop skills of understanding and to consider some questions put to them from an accompanying teacher's workbook, and/or the children create their own questions.
3 The teacher facilitates their discussion making use of exercises, structures and questions from the teacher's workbook.
4 At each session, they repeat the above procedure with the next section of text, carrying forward previous discussions.

P4/wC (Philosophy for/with Children)

1 A stimulus is presented, e.g. a picture book.
2 Questions are formulated by the children in response to the stimulus.
3 The questions are listed and sorted (see Idea 97), and a question is selected by the children.
4 This question then becomes the basis of an enquiry, facilitated by the teacher.

CoPI (Community of Philosophical Inquiry)

1 A stimulus is presented, e.g. an item.
2 Questions are formulated by the children in response to the stimulus.
3 The teacher chooses the question with the most philosophical potential and it becomes the basis for an enquiry.
4 The following template is provided for the participants to be able to contribute, ensuring dialectical progress and impartiality: 'I agree/disagree with [pupil's name – usually a made-up pseudonym] when he/she said... because...'
5 The enquiry is carefully facilitated to ensure the discussion remains appropriately philosophical.

PhiE (Philosophical Enquiry)

1 A stimulus is presented, e.g. a story, drawn from or inspired by the philosophical canon.
2 A carefully chosen task question (Idea 2) is asked by the teacher or children that brings the class to a philosophical issue around the stimulus.
3 An enquiry is facilitated where the facilitator plays a structural role in ensuring that the intellectual demands of the philosophical enquiry are attempted to be met, using questioning techniques in this book.

All these approaches share a commitment to doing philosophy with children through conversation (loosely in the Socratic tradition) and giving the children ownership of the enquiry. PhiE and CoPI are primarily committed to exploring philosophical issues and topics according to reason while P4/wC aims to attain certain social and political ends, such as promoting good citizenship.

Bonus idea ★

PHiE: www.philosophy-foundation.org

P4/wC in the UK: www.sapere.org.uk

Lipman/Sharp P4C: Institute for the Advancement of Philosophy for Children (IAPC): www.montclair.edu/cehs/academics/centers-and-institutes/iapc/

McCall's CoPI: *Transforming Thinking* (Routledge, 2009)

www.thinkingspace.org.uk

www.thephilosophyman.com

https://www.teachingchildrenphilosophy.org/

Enquiry ideas around questioning

'Questioning is questioning questions, too.' (Nine-year-old pupil)

Here are some simple enquiry ideas you can use as starters to get your class (and yourself!) thinking around questions.

Teaching tip

Remember to anchor (see Idea 37) to the main task questions.

Enquiry idea 1

This enquiry uses the Kokey Hokey method (Idea 63).

Task question 1a: What is a question? (Try 'Break the circle' on this, see Idea 10.)

Task question 1b: Are the following questions?

- It remains an open question whether or not we are alone in the universe.
- Would you mind putting the knife down?
- Could I see your passport please? (*Said at passport control*)
- 'To be or not to be: that is the question.' (*Hamlet*)
- How are you today?
- ?

Task question 1c: If a question is [insert suggestions from task question 1a], then are the above questions?

Enquiry idea 2

What would the world be like without questions?

This question is a good general-purpose questioning structure for enquiries: 'What would the world be like without X?'

Enquiry idea 3

Task question: Do all questions have answers? How about these?

- How many stars are there?
- Do aliens exist?
- How many grains of sand are there in the world?
- Who is the best singer in the world?
- Is there life after death?
- Does this question have an answer?
- Is the mind the same as the brain?
- Are toves slithy? How do toves gyre and gimble? What is a wabe? (See *Jabberwocky* by Lewis Carroll.)

Taking it further

These enquiries would work well if used within a philosophy approach (see Idea 90).

Enquiry idea 4

Use picture books based around questions and questioning to run a P4C community of inquiry (Ideas 31 and 90), such as:

- *Why?* Lindsay Camp and Tony Ross (2008)
- *Would You Rather?* John Burningham (1994)
- *Also an Octopus,* Maggie Tokuda-Hall and Benji Davies (2017)
- *What Makes Me a Me?* Ben Faulks and David Tazzyman (2017)
- *The Black Box,* Albert B. Carr (1969)

Socratic circles

'Well, I was watching the whole thing from a *third* circle.' (Baroness Warnock after silently taking part in a Socratic circle enquiry)

This is a powerful, all-purpose, metacognitive pedagogical strategy that has been named after Socrates, presumably because of similarities to his philosophical method.

Teaching tip

This is a child-centred approach to discussions, one in which you should 'take a backseat' and perform the role of facilitator or coach.

Taking it further

Read *Socratic Circles* by Matt Copeland (2005) and see also the related method of Socratic seminars (see Wikipedia), both of which develop a metacognitive 'outside eye' on one's thinking.

The basic principle behind Socratic circles is that there are two circles: an 'inner circle' and an 'outer circle', like so:

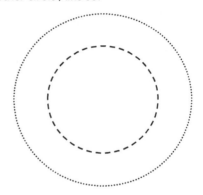

The inner circle represents those involved in a first-order discussion about a topic, question or issue, such as when the children in your class are having a discussion around a question they have been asked. The outer circle represents those who are not concerned with the question *per se* but with the second-order question of *the discussion itself*.

One way to think of this is to imagine a film being made of the children having their discussion and then a group of educators watching the film to discuss the discussion. What the outer circle concerns itself with regarding the discussion will vary depending on the outer circle's aims and objectives. They could be thinking about how well the group is speaking and listening, thinking critically, the quality of their questioning, or about how well the facilitator/teacher is doing, and so on. Key to the outer-circle attitude is that no matter what criteria they are considering they will be thinking about the *quality of the discussion*.

Socratic circles are useful in classrooms for getting children to think about the quality of what they are doing and for helping children to develop their own question-asking (see Idea 94).

The Socratic classroom

One more formal way to proceed is to set the classroom up in a Socratic circle format for certain tasks and activities. This involves forming two circles of chairs. Those children sitting in the inner circle participate in doing the task, such as conducting a discussion around a central question. Those children sitting in the outer circle observe the inner circle activity and are given certain, specific tasks. Often it is easier for the outer circle to perform these tasks with a piece of paper and a pencil, so that they can make notes. These tasks may include:

- listening out for reasons/arguments
- listening out for things they agree/disagree with
- formulating questions for the inner circle
- evaluating the discussion.

The Socratic pupil(s)

Another way of using this method is to assign certain outer circle roles to one or more children. They could be given a piece of paper and pencil and asked to formulate questions to ask the group or you could ask a certain member of the group to concept-map the discussion, summarising it in their own words.

20 questions

'A tomato is not a vegetable; it's got seeds!' (Ten-year-old 'Smart Alec')

This well-known game is great for encouraging children to think about questions.

1 Explain the rules and the difference between the categories 'animal', 'vegetable' and 'mineral'.
2 One person ('the thinker') thinks of an object, any object, and tells the teacher what it is.
3 The thinker should state to the class whether it is an animal, vegetable or mineral.
4 The others now have a maximum of 20 questions to ask in order to ascertain what the object is. The thinker can only answer with the following responses:
   • 'Yes'
   • 'No'
   • 'Usually'
   • 'Sometimes'
   • 'Rarely'
   • 'I don't know'
5 Keep a tally of the number of questions asked and record any information gained on the board. Ask, periodically, 'What, if anything, do we know about the object after that question?'
6 Once 20 questions have been asked, each person gets *one chance* to say what they think the object is.
7 Reveal the object.

Reflect on the game with children once it is finished:

1 Ask pupils:
   a) Was their answer(s) close?
   b) Was their questioning effective?
   c) How could their questioning be improved in subsequent games?

d) Were there any questions that were particularly effective or useful? (Which were they, and why?)
e) Were there any questions that were not so effective or useful? (Which were they, and why? Discuss.)

2 Write the following on the board (I use these, rather than questions that came up in the game, so as not to single out children's questions for evaluation):

A) Is it edible?
B) Is it a carrot?

Ask:

a) Are these questions good questions in a game of '20 questions'?
b) And if the answer *was* a carrot, would B be a good question?

3 If the answer to a question is 'No', does that mean that it was a bad question to ask?
4 What makes a good/bad question in '20 questions'?

Taking it further

The game could be taken up a level by:

- introducing abstract entities
- reducing the number of questions
- challenging them to improve on their earlier record.

Questions from children

'Do you paint your hair grey?' (Six-year-old's question to me)

Thinking about *your* questions is one thing, but it is also important to consider how to get the *children* to ask questions.

As any teacher will have experienced, asking your class, 'Are there any questions?' is often met with silence or goes in a completely different direction. This idea will provide some ways to get children asking better questions.

Philosophy for Children (P4C)

P4C is a pedagogy (see Idea 90) that has developed many ways of getting children to come up with their own questions. These methods and approaches can also be used outside of P4C to help children generate questions for themselves. Notable among them is 'The question quadrant' (Idea 97).

Question structures and starters

One problem with asking children to ask questions of each other in discussions or lessons is that they often use a question to make a point: 'Why do you think it has to be X, because I think that...'. One way to help them with this is to (when appropriate) stipulate that *they are not allowed to make their own point when questioning each other*. Another is to provide them with question structures and starters such as those you'll find in Idea 41. Having these structures up on the classroom wall serves two functions: reminding you what opening-up strategies there are that you could use, and also something to draw the children's attention to when asking them to question each other.

Hand signals or cards

Try giving the children a hand signal for asking a question, such as making a 'Q' or '?' with their hands. This can be done by making a circle with the thumb and forefinger of one hand and a line through it with the forefinger of the other for 'Q', or a 'C' shape with the thumb and forefinger of one hand and line under it to form a '?' with the forefinger of the other. This might help identify a question when it is relevant rather than getting to the question too late for any sequential flow in the discussion. Alternatively, you might want to make them each a question card (a card with a question mark on) to hold up when they have a question. Cards can be made for other kinds of response, too, such as agree/disagree cards, 'add to' cards ('I agree and...'), 'qualify' cards ('I agree but...') and so on. Thanks to Andrew Day for these suggestions.

Problematise to motivate

A colleague at The Philosophy Foundation, Andrew Day, has identified a very important aspect to how one inspires questioning in the children. Here is my own formulation of Andrew's principle:

Teach in such a way that you inspire questions from the children, the answers to which are what you need to teach.

The example he gives is to do with the teaching of punctuation. First of all, Andrew researched the history of punctuation to see what need(s) its introduction met. He discovered that it was first used by ancient Greek dramatists to indicate pauses in speech to help the players with their delivery. This inspired the following lesson plan. He wrote a short dramatic dialogue for the children to perform but left out all the punctuation. It was written in such a way that without any punctuation it was difficult to make sense of. This created a need that punctuation could solve, making the introduction of punctuation to the children relevant, necessary and practical. (See also Idea 26.)

Emergent questions

Often, the best questions arise organically during a discussion rather than before it. See Idea 5.

10 questions

'I *know* 18 is the right answer. It *has* to be because it's even, it's lower than 20 and it's in the nine times table.' (Eight-year-old girl reasoning to certainty)

This is a similar game to '20 questions', called '10 questions'. It is based around numbers.

Teaching tip

The key questioning strategy for this and other logic games is 'if-ing, anchoring and opening up' (Idea 43) and 'The Question X' (Idea 17).

Taking it further

For more logic games see Robert Fisher's *Games for Thinking* (1997) and The Philosophy Foundation website: www. philosophy-foundation. org (members section – which is free).

1 Decide on a number range (e.g. between 1 and 10, 1 and 100, 1 and 1,000, and so on). This will depend on the children's age, ability and experience.
2 Write a number down within your chosen range, remember it and put it in a sealed envelope.
3 Tell the children that they have only ten questions to ask you in order to establish what the number is, to which the answer has to be either 'Yes' or 'No'.
4 Keep a tally of the number of questions used and any information gleaned recorded on the board for all to see.
5 Once the ten questions have all been used, allow each child to say which number they think is in the envelope and ask them to say why they have chosen their number. Ask them how certain they are (from 1 to 10) and allow a short discussion around this, particularly inviting reasons for and against any suggested answers.

Reflect on the game using suggestions in Idea 93.

Question train!

'This is one time where the question should be as long and as complicated as possible.'

This is an adaptation of an activity (among many others) in David Shapiro's *Plato Was Wrong!* (2012). It provides a good opportunity to explain how questions, as a form, are structured.

1 Stand the class or group around in a circle.
2 Ask them to create a question by adding one word at a time as they go around the circle successively. For example, the first person may say, 'Who', then the second, 'is', then the third, 'the' and so on. It must have the form of a question and it must make sense. So, not, 'Who sausage when could curve nowhere?' but perhaps, 'Is there an end to the universe?' or even 'Is there a tired Wednesday?' (This makes sense structurally though the content is problematic – but it could be a good discussion starter!)
3 When the question is complete (it makes sense and could end) the person whose go it is claps to indicate that the question is finished. It is their choice whether they clap or not. If they don't, it has to continue until the next opportunity for a clap.
4 If a clap is made, count how many words there are.
5 Play again, this time aiming to beat the number of words in the question. But remember: it has to be a question and it has to make sense.

Teaching tip

Generate questions for discussion, stipulating at the start what kinds of question they must try to formulate: Science? Maths? Philosophy? For philosophy or P4C questions stipulate that any nouns be *abstract nouns*. If they don't know what these are, then introduce them. To extend this, you can take on the role of getting the children 'out' by being very strict about whether the question makes sense or is the kind of question that you have stipulated, 'How's that an X question?' They then must argue for its inclusion: 'It IS an X question because...'.

The question quadrant

'If only we could teach [the pupils] to ask better questions...' (Philip Cam)

This is a useful (and adaptable) method for teachers and children to sort questions once they have been formulated. It was developed by Philip Cam in his book *Twenty Thinking Tools* (2006). Originally devised for use with communities of inquiry and P4C, it has much wider application in the hands of inventive teachers.

Teaching tip

Cam suggests laying the question quadrant out on the floor with the labels on pieces of card.

Traditionally, the question quadrant splits questions up into the following:

Textual questions

(Reading comprehension) | (Literacy speculation)

Closed questions —————— **Open questions**

(Factual knowledge) | (Inquiry)

Intellectual questions

Adapted from: Cam, P. (2006) *Twenty Thinking Tools*. Melbourne: ACER Press, p. 34.

This is fine for teachers to sort questions, but it might be difficult for pupils to approach, so Cam suggests using the following or similar alternatives for them:

- **Closed:** 'There is only one right answer.'
- **Open:** 'There may be many possibilities.'
- **Reading comprehension:** 'Look and see questions' or 'The answer is in the book.'
- **Factual knowledge:** 'Ask an expert' or 'Ask someone who knows the answer.'
- **Literary speculation:** 'Use your imagination.'
- **Inquiry:** 'Thinking questions' or 'You really have to think about it.'

My own suggested procedure for using the quadrant (combined with 'Think, pair, square, share' in Idea 62) is:

1 Each child formulates a question in response to a stimulus.
2 In pairs, they should decide on one question based on provided criteria.
3 In fours, they should decide on one question.
4 The chosen questions should be submitted and written up for all to see.
5 These should then be sorted according to the question quadrant you have devised. Reasons should be provided for categorisations.
6 Move to whatever further procedure is appropriate for your teaching ends.

Taking it further

You may want to adapt this to suit your teaching ends. For example, you might want the children to sort questions into subjects, e.g. science/history/philosophy/other, or into sub-categories of one category, e.g. different types of factual question (see Idea 8). Be creative!

Questions only!

'**Rosencrantz:** Are you counting that?
Guildenstern: What?
R: Are you counting that?
G: Foul! No repetitions.'
(From *Rosencrantz and Guildenstern Are Dead* by Tom Stoppard, 1973)

This is a classroom adaptation of a game for pairs in *Games for Thinking* by Robert Fisher (1997), in which you will find more question games.

Taking it further

Defender: Have one pupil or group defend a statement and another challenge the statement with *only* questions that must be answered (see 'Proper consideration' in Idea 19).

1 Split the class into two groups.
2 Provide them with a setting, e.g. 'You're at the supermarket' or 'You're on the moon.'
3 Flip a coin to decide which team starts.
4 Someone – anyone! – from the team asks a question of the other group.
5 Turn to the other team for someone in that team to respond to the question with another question.
6 Alternate between both teams in this fashion.
7 If they do not answer with a question (or an acceptable question), or if they don't answer quickly enough, someone from the team should sit down.

As they play more and get the hang of the game, introduce more stringent rules. For example, to decide if a question is acceptable, you might insist that:

• The questions connect to the question asked, e.g. 'Do you like the moon?' or 'What do you mean by "like"?'
• The questions are not simply repeats of the question asked – not, for example, 'Why are you here?'; 'Why are YOU here?'
• They do not use rhetorical questions ('How can you like the moon when it's uninhabitable?') This class of question is tricky because, though it has a question form, it is not being used to ask a question, but to make a point.

Walls and boxes

'A box can't be bigger on the inside!' (Doctor Who's companion)

Have a 'question box' for the classroom or set up a 'question/thinking/strategy wall' or 'corner', a place where questions, thinking tools or learning strategies can be displayed, deposited, collected and/or distributed.

Question box

You can use a box to:

- put a selection of prepared questions in
- collect questions from the class
- vet question, e.g. to find inappropriate ones before reading out to the class
- anonymise questions gathered
- randomly select a question to discuss/answer.

Anonymous questions/answers

Sometimes you want honest answers that you may not get, such as when asking ethical questions (Idea 12). This might be because the pupils are self-conscious, or they think they might get into trouble for answering a question honestly. If so, you can ask them to write down an answer on a piece of paper without putting their name on it.

Walls

This could be a space on the wall with a central question/topic/stimulus written up and a sticky note pad on the side. Allow pupils to write their questions/answers on the sticky notes and then stick them on the wall. A 'question wall' could also be a place to put question starters and structures (see Idea 94). I have made some suggestions throughout this book for when to use your question/strategy walls/boxes (e.g. in Ideas 48, 58 and 100).

Teaching tip

Once questions have been collected, they need sorting – see Idea 97.

Bonus idea ★

Leonardo Da Vinci's 10 Questions: this well-known renaissance man would make a list of questions about something that interested him. Take any stimulus, such as a cube of ice, and ask each person or group to write ten questions in response to the stimulus *that they must try to answer.* (Idea taken from *Think Like Da Vinci* by Michael Gelb, 2009.)

Metacognitive questions

'"Learning to learn" makes no sense; it's like "eating to eat".' (Twitter user, *Times Educational Supplement*)

'Metacognition' is a word that you hear a lot in education circles even though it's not always clear what people mean by it. However, it is a useful term once understood. 'Cognition' is to do with thoughts/thinking and knowledge, and 'meta' means 'outside' or 'beyond'. Sometimes people describe metacognition as 'thinking about thinking' or 'learning to learn'. This is helpful but I would add: 'in order to improve'.

Teaching tip

Have a place for any strategies you've shown the children on your wall (Idea 99), so that when you ask the fourth question you can direct them to the 'strategy wall' to help.

Taking it further

Once a class is used to answering questions 1 to 4, you might want to ask the following question *before* a task question: 'How do you think we can best answer the question (or solve the problem)?' Then, once they've attempted to answer the task question go through questions 1 to 4 to have them evaluate how well they think they did.

The stages of metacognition are:
- **Be aware!** E.g. 'I am/they are confused!'
- **Monitor!** E.g. 'What happens when I am/they are confused?'
- **Analyse!** E.g. 'Why am I/are they confused? Should I/they be? Do I/they understand?'
- **Evaluate!** E.g. 'Is my/their being confused a vice or a virtue?' 'Is their confusion due to something I've done?'
- **Strategise!** E.g. 'What can I do to tackle my/their confusion?'

It is important to think of metacognition and the use of metacognitive questions as something you direct both towards the children and yourself. Eventually, you should aim to have the children ask these kinds of questions of themselves. (See also Idea 28.) Here are some useful progressive questions to ask yourself or the children:

1 Have we answered the question/problem? If not, why not?
2 Have we got closer to (made progress towards) answering the question/problem? If so, in what way? If not, why not?
3 How might we better answer/get closer to answering the question/problem?
4 Are there any specific strategies we might employ to do so? How can we use them?

References

Anderson, L. W. and Krathwohl, D. R. (2001) *A Taxonomy for Learning, Teaching and Assessing: A Revision of Bloom's Taxonomy of Educational Objectives: Complete Edition*. Harlow: Longman.

Baggini, J. (2008) *The Duck that Won the Lottery*. London: Granta.

Bartlett, J. and Miller, C. (2011) 'Truth, lies and the internet: a report into young people's digital fluency'. Demos.

Biesta, G. (2017) 'Touching the soul? Exploring an alternative outlook for philosophical work with children and young people', *Childhood and Philosophy*, 13, (28), 415–452.

Birch, D. (2014) *Provocations: Philosophy for Secondary Schools*. Carmarthen: Crown House Publishing.

Booth, E. (2001) *The Everyday Work of Art*. Lincoln, NE: iUniverse.com.

Bowker, M. H. (2010) 'Teaching students to ask questions instead of answering them.' *Thought and Action,* 26, (1), 127–134.

Buckley, J. (2012) *Thinkers' Games* (2nd edn.). Chelmsford: One Slice Books.

Buckley, J. and Bigglestone, T. (2016) *Philosophy Circles*. Philosophy Man Ltd.

Burningham, J. (1994) *Would You Rather?* London: Red Fox.

Cam, P. (2006) *Twenty Thinking Tools*. Melbourne: ACER Press.

Camp, L. and Ross, T. (2008) *Why?* London: Andersen.

Campbell-Harris, S. (2017) 'How to teach controversy in the classroom', *Innovate My School,* http://www.innovatemyschool.com/ideas/too-close-to-home-how-to-handle-controversy-in-the-classroom

Carr, A. B. (1969) *The Black Box*. Prentice Hall.

Cohen, M. (2004) *Wittgenstein's Beetle and Other Classic Thought Experiments*. Oxford: Wiley-Blackwell.

Concern Worldwide, *Primary Debating Handbook,* https://www.concern.net/sites/default/files/media/page/primary_debating_handbook_a5_updated.pdf

Copeland, M. (2005) *Socratic Circles*. Portland, ME: Stenhouse.

Dabell, J. (2017) 'Fermi questions', *Teacher Toolkit*, https://www.teachertoolkit.co.uk/2017/04/28/fermiquestions/

Descartes, R. (1641) *Meditations on The First Philosophy*, in R. Ariew and D. Cress (eds.), *Meditations, Objections, and Replies*. Indianapolis, IN: Hackett.

Dillon, J. T. (1994) *Using Discussion in Classrooms*. Milton Keynes: Open University Press.

Dimbylow, L. 'How to help your child develop study skills', *The School Run*, https://www.theschoolrun.com/primary-study-skills

Faulks, B. and Tazzyman, B. (2017) *What Makes Me a Me?* London: Bloomsbury.

Fisher, R. (1997) *Games for Thinking*. Oxford: Nash Pollock Publishing.

Gallagher, J. J. and Ascher, M. J. (1963) 'A preliminary report on analyses of classroom interaction', *Merrill-Palmer Quarterly*, 9, (1), 183–194.

Gardner, S. (1995) 'Inquiry is no mere conversation', *Critical and Creative Thinking*, 3, (2), 38–49.

Gelb, M. (2009) *Think Like Da Vinci: 7 Easy Steps to Boosting Your Everyday Genius* (revised edn). London: Harper Collins.

Gilbert, I. (2007) *The Little Book of Thunks*. Carmarthen: Crown House Publishing.

Haynes, J. and Murris, K. (2012) *Picturebooks, Pedagogy and Philosophy*. Abingdon: Routledge.

Kagan, S., Kagan, M. and Kagan, L. (2015) *59 Kagan Structures: Proven Engagement Strategies*. San Clemente, CA: Kagan.

Kessels, J., Boers, E. and Mostert, P. (2009) *Free Space: Field Guide to Conversations*. Los Angeles, CA: Boom.

McCall, C. (2009) *Transforming Thinking*. Abingdon: Routledge.

Michaels, S., O'Connor, C. and Resnick, L. B. (2008) 'Deliberative discourse idealized and realized: accountable talk in the classroom and civic life', *Studies in Philosophy and Education*, 27, (4), 283–297.

Morgan, N. and Saxton, J. (2006) *Asking Better Questions* (2nd edn.). Markham, ON: Pembroke Publishers Ltd.

Muruzábal Lamberti, P. (2018) 'Apprentices of listening', *The Philosophy Foundation* blog, www.philosophy-foundation.org/blog/apprentices-of-listening

National Literacy Trust (2017) 'Fake news and critical literacy introductory resources', https://literacytrust.org.uk/resources/fake-news-and-critical-literacy/

Nottingham, J., 'Learning Pit', www.jamesnottingham.co.uk/learning-pit/

Orwell, G. (1946) 'Politics and the English language', in *Essays*. London: Penguin Classics.

Philosophy Now Radio Show (2011) 'Primary school philosophy', https://philosophynow.org/podcasts/Primary_School_Philosophy

Plato. *Euthyphro* and *Meno*, in J. M. Cooper (ed.), *Plato Complete Works*. Indianapolis, IN: Hackett.

Quigley, A., Muijs, D. and Stringer, E. (2018) 'Metacognition and self-regulated learning: guidance report', *Education Endowment Foundation*, https://educationendowmentfoundation.org.uk/tools/guidance-reports/metacognition-and-self-regulated-learning

Rees, J. and Sullivan, W. (2008) *Clean Language: Revealing Metaphors and Opening Minds.* Carmarthen: Crown House Publishing.

Robinson, M. (2013) *Trivium 21c: Preparing Young People for the Future with Lessons from the Past*. Carmarthen: Independent Thinking Press.

Sayers, D. (2017) *The Lost Tools of Learning*. Louisville, KY: GLH Publishing.

Sendak, M. (2000) *Where the Wild Things Are*. London: Red Fox.

Shapiro, D. (2012) *Plato Was Wrong!* Lanham, MD: Rowman & Littlefield Education.

Sprod, T. (2016) 'In out, in out, shake it all about', *The Philosophy Foundation blog*, https://www.philosophy-foundation.org/blog/in-out-in-out-shake-it-all-about

Sternberg, R. J. and Grigorenko, E. (1997) 'Are cognitive styles still in style?' *American Psychologist*, 52, (7), 700–712.

Sternberg, R. J., Kaufman, J. C. and Grigorenko, E. (2008) *Applied Intelligence*. Cambridge: Cambridge University Press.

Stoppard, T. (1973) *Rosencrantz and Guildenstern Are Dead*. New York, NY: Grove Press.

Taggart, A. (2011) 'Pete Worley of The Philosophy Foundation asks, "How many things are there?"', https://andrewjtaggart.com/2011/11/

Tittle, P. (2004) *What If... Collected Thought Experiments in Philosophy*. Abingdon: Routledge.

Tokuda-Hall, M. and Davies, B. (2017) *Also an Octopus*. London: Walker Books.

Ungerer, T. (2009) *The Three Robbers*. London: Phaidon Press.

Velthuijs, M. (1997) *Frog is a Hero*. London: Andersen.

Warburton, N. (2007) *Thinking from A to Z* (3rd edn.). Abingdon: Routledge.

Wartenberg, T. (2014) *Big Ideas for Little Kids*. Lanham, MD: Rowman & Littlefield Education.

West, A. (2015) 'Philosophy saved me from poverty and drugs: that's why I teach it to kids', *The Guardian*, 19 November 2015, https://www.theguardian.com/commentisfree/2015/nov/19/philosophy-poverty-drugs-kids-young-people

Weston, A. (2018) *A Rulebook for Arguments* (5th edn.). Cambridge, MA: Hackett Publishing.

Wiggins, K. (2016) 'Carol Dweck: "The whole idea of growth mindset is to say yes they can"', *Times Educational Supplement*, 26 June 2015, https://www.tes.com/news/carol-dweck-whole-idea-growth-mindset-say-yes-they-can

Worley, P. (2011a) 'What can university philosophy learn from primary philosophy?', Lecture delivered at St Mary's University, www.academia.edu/36758580/What_can_university_philosophy_learn_from_primary_philosophy

Worley, P. (2011b) *The If Machine*. London: Bloomsbury Education.

Worley, P., (ed.) (2012) *The Philosophy Shop: Ideas, Activities and Questions to Get People, Young and Old, Thinking Philosophically*. Carmarthen: Independent Thinking Press.

Worley, P. (2015a) *40 Lessons to Get Children Thinking*. London: Bloomsbury Education.

Worley, P. (2015b) 'Open thinking, closed questioning: two kinds of open and closed question', *Journal of Philosophy in Schools*, 2, (2), https://www.ojs.unisa.edu.au/index.php/jps/article/view/1269

Worley, P. (2016a) 'Ariadne's Clew: absence and presence in the facilitation of philosophical conversations', *Journal of Philosophy in Schools*, 3, (2).

Worley, P. (2016b) 'How to introduce critical thinking into your classroom', *Innovate My School*, http://www.innovatemyschool.com/ideas/how-to-introduce-critical-thinking-skills-into-your-classroom

Worley, P. (2018) 'Dissonance: disagreement and critical thinking in P4/wC', in E. Duthie, F. García Moriyón and R. Robles Loro (eds.), *Family Resemblances: Current Trends in Philosophy for Children*. Madrid.

Yenawine, P. (2013) *Visual Thinking Strategies: Using Art to Deepen Learning Across School Disciplines*. Cambridge, MA: Harvard Education Press.

Zwozdiak-Myers, P. (2012) *The Teacher's Reflective Practice Handbook: Becoming an Extended Professional Through Capturing Evidence-Informed Practice*. Abingdon: Routledge.